JOURNEYS

Quick  Start Pacing Guide

4

Contents

JOURNEYS OVERVIEW

Program Consultants

Teach with confidence. Journeys is a research-based, comprehensive English Language Arts program developed by literacy experts and backed by proven results.

Shervaughnna Anderson Director of the California Reading and Literature Project at UCLA. Ms. Anderson brings an extensive knowledge of coaching and has experience in establishing and nurturing professional learning communities. She is a former teacher, coach, and site and district-level administrator.

Before joining the UCLA Reading Program, Ms. Anderson was a K-12 English Language Arts Consultant at the Los Angeles County Office of Education. She has experience working with diverse student-populations throughout the United States and abroad. In addition, she has served on state committees addressing English Language Arts instruction, English Learners, and instructional practices for African American students.

Martha Hougen National consultant, presenter, researcher, and author. Areas of expertise include differentiating instruction for students with learning difficulties, including those with learning disabilities and dyslexia, and teacher and leader preparation improvement. Dr. Hougen received a BS in Education from University of Wisconsin at Madison, an MEd from American University, and a PhD in Educational Administration from University of Texas at Austin. She has taught at the middle school through graduate levels. Recently her focus has been on working with teacher educators to enhance teacher and leader preparation to better meet the needs of all students.

In addition to peer-reviewed articles, curricular documents, and presentations, Dr. Hougen has published two college textbooks: *The Fundamentals of Literacy Assessment and Instruction PreK–6* (2012) and *The Fundamentals of Literacy Assessment and Instruction 6–12* (2014).

Carol Jago Teacher of English in middle and high school for 32 years, and director of the California Reading and Literature Project at UCLA. Past president of the National Council of Teachers of English, Ms. Jago served as AP* Literature content advisor for the College Board and now serves on its English Academic Advisory committee. She edits the journal of the California Association of Teachers of English, *California English,* and served on the planning committee for the 2009 NAEP Reading Framework and the 2011 NAEP Writing Framework. She is the recipient of the IRA Thought Leader in Adolescent Literacy Award.

Ms. Jago has published six books with Heinemann, including *With Rigor for All* and *Papers, Papers, Papers.* She has also published four books on contemporary multicultural authors for NCTE's High School Literature Series.

Ms. Jago received her BA in English from the University of California, Santa Barbara, and MA Secondary Credential from the University of Southern California, Los Angeles.

Erik Palmer Veteran teacher and education consultant based in Denver, Colorado. Dr. Palmer's areas of focus include improving oral communication, promoting technology in classroom presentations, and updating instruction through the use of digital tools. He has worked with school districts in the United States and Mexico in the area of teaching speaking skills to 21st-century learners. He has also worked with private and public schools as a consultant on two topics: teaching oral communication, and showing non-tech-savvy teachers practical ways to use technology in the classroom. He is a frequent presenter and keynote speaker at state, regional, and national conferences of education professionals.

Dr. Palmer holds a BA from Oberlin College and an MA in curriculum and instruction from the University of Colorado. He is the author of *Well Spoken: Teaching Speaking to All Students* and *Digitally Speaking: How to Improve Student Presentations.*

Shane Templeton Foundation Professor Emeritus of Literacy Studies at the University of Nevada, Reno. A former classroom teacher at the primary and secondary levels, Dr. Templeton's research has focused on developmental word knowledge in elementary, middle, and high school students. He is co-author of *Words Their Way; Vocabulary Their Way: Word Study for Middle and Secondary Students; Words Their Way with Struggling Readers, Grades 4–12;* and *Words Their Way with English Learners.* His other books include *Teaching the Integrated Language Arts* and *Children's Literacy: Contexts for Meaningful Learning.*

Since 1987, Dr. Templeton has been a member of the Usage Panel of The American Heritage® Dictionary. He is an educational consultant on *The American Heritage Children's Dictionary* and wrote the foreword to the recently published *Curious George's Dictionary.* He is also a senior author of *Houghton Mifflin Reading; Houghton Mifflin Harcourt Spelling and Vocabulary;* co-author of *Houghton Mifflin Harcourt English;* and co-author of *Earobics® REACH.*

Program Consultants

MaryEllen Vogt Distinguished Professor Emerita of Education at California State University, Long Beach. Dr. Vogt has been a classroom teacher, reading specialist, special education specialist, curriculum coordinator, and university teacher educator, and served as president of the International Reading Association. Her research interests include improving comprehension in the content areas, teacher change and development, and content literacy and language acquisition for English learners.

Dr. Vogt has provided professional development in all fifty US states, and in nine other countries. She was inducted into the California Reading Hall of Fame, and received her university's Distinguished Faculty Teaching Award. With a doctorate from the University of California, Berkeley, Dr. Vogt is a co-author of 15 publications, including *Houghton Mifflin Reading; 99 MORE Ideas and Activities for Teaching English Learners with the SIOP Model;* and *Reading Specialist and Literacy Coaches in the Real World,* Third Edition.

Sheila Valencia Professor of Language, Literacy, and Culture at the University of Washington, where she teaches and conducts research in the areas of literacy assessment, instruction, policy, and teacher development. Dr. Valencia began her career as a 6th-grade teacher in an urban district in New York City, followed by several years as a teacher in a rural district, and then as director of a reading clinic for students with reading difficulties. She went back into public education for six years before returning to academia as a teacher educator and researcher.

Dr. Valencia's work has appeared in numerous journals, including *Reading Research Quarterly, The Reading Teacher, Elementary School Journal, Journal of Literacy Research,* and *Journal of Teacher Education.* She is also a co-author of *Houghton Mifflin Reading.* Dr. Valencia has served on national, state, and local assessment committees to improve reading assessment systems and policies, and was the 2009–2010 chair of the IRA Assessment Committee. In 2008, she was inducted into the International Reading Association Reading Hall of Fame. Dr. Valencia received her MEd from SUNY Buffalo and a PhD from the University of Colorado.

SPECIAL CONSULTANT

Irene Fountas Former classroom teacher, language arts specialist, and consultant in school districts across the nation and abroad. Ms. Fountas works extensively in the literacy education field and directs the Literacy Collaborative in the School of Education at Lesley University. She spends her time providing training to literacy coaches and key administrators who play roles in teacher development and school improvement. Along with her co-author, Gay Su Pinnell, she has developed the country's most widely used standard for leveling text for small group instruction. They have authored many books, including *Guided Reading, Teaching for Comprehending and Fluency,* and *When Readers Struggle.* Their latest publication is *The Continuum of Literacy Learning, Grades PreK–8: A Guide to Teaching.*

Dr. Fountas is the recipient of the Greater Boston Council of the International Reading Association's Celebrate Literacy Award. She is a consulting author for *Lessons in Literacy* from Great Source, *Houghton Mifflin Leveled Readers, Houghton Mifflin Vocabulary Readers,* and *Houghton Mifflin Science Leveled Readers.*

Program Overview

Journeys provides effective and efficient initial instruction, progress-monitoring and scaffolded support for all students, and a robust mechanism for intervention.

Instruct

Teacher's Edition
Delivers systematic, research-based instruction, integrated English language support, ongoing formative assessment, and differentiated instruction daily

Student Book
High-quality literary and informational texts in multiple genres for close reading and responding; vocabulary, grammar, and writing activities; and performance tasks

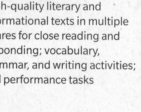

Language Workshop
Small group support to help English learners quickly increase their level of English proficiency

Interactive Lessons Digital lessons in writing, speaking, and listening provide students with opportunities to reinforce vital communications skills independently

Write-In Reader
Provides close reading practice and an on-ramp to each Anchor Text

Trade Books
Offer students rich literary and informational content on a variety of topics

HMH Decoding Power: Intensive Reading Instruction
Systematically builds the critical foundational skills that many struggling readers need for reading success

Leveled Readers
Provide additional reading practice for all students

Support

Intervene

Program Philosophy

Journeys is a research-based, rigorous, comprehensive English Language Arts program designed to provide all students with a path to achieving success with grade-level instructional standards. Inspired by five key themes, *Journeys* empowers and motivates students to develop college and career readiness as broadly literate, increasingly independent lifelong learners.

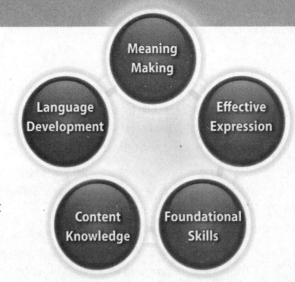

Meaning Making

Students interact with and produce text, participate in collaborative discussions, engage in research, and make presentations for the purpose of making meaning.

Journeys provides a framework in which to develop students' abilities to make meaning of texts through close reading and analysis, listening comprehension, writing to sources using text evidence, communicating ideas, and responding to the ideas of peers.

Meaning Making supports include

- Anchor Texts and Paired Selections that are intellectually challenging and worthy of multiple reads

- Text X-Ray teaching tool to help the teacher zoom in on key ideas and language points and prepare to support and challenge his or her individual students

- *my*Notebook annotation tool to encourage direct engagement with the language and ideas of the texts

- Reader's Notebook for making critical thinking and text analysis visible

- Trade Books for extended readings to gain information, endurance, and appreciation of the power of literature

- Integrated English Language Support to scaffold access for learners at diverse levels of English proficiency

- Differentiated instruction built into every lesson, as part of the core instructional routine—not as an afterthought—to give all students opportunities to engage with challenging ideas and language

- Write-In Reader for practice with close reading parallel texts that help readers "ramp up" to the Anchor Text, with a Reading Detective feature every week to motivate and scaffold close reading

- Teacher Read Alouds for engaging in listening comprehension

- Performance Tasks and Assessments for practice in synthesizing multiple texts

Language Development

Academic language development is critical for students' ability to learn, think, and express.

The systematic, carefully sequenced instructional design of *Journeys* guides students to use language to acquire and convey meaning effectively. Rich academic language instruction through daily vocabulary, grammar, and writing lessons is delivered in meaningful contexts and provides appropriate levels of support for all students, particularly culturally and linguistically diverse learners, to help them meet the language demands of school and beyond.

Language Development supports include

- Language Detective features with every Anchor Text to facilitate analysis of the author's language use and how it builds meaning

- How English Works features in each lesson to help teachers use the texts to build linguistic awareness and skills

- Language Workshop, a complete, rigorous, systematic program for ELD that builds into and from the core program to enable language learners to stretch to greater proficiency in academic English

- Vocabulary Readers to provide additional context for the use of academic vocabulary from the lesson

- *my*WordList eBook tool that enables students to collect unfamiliar words as they read in order to build a personal, ongoing word list, thereby managing their own vocabulary development

- Domain-Specific Vocabulary lessons that focus on content-area vocabulary from history/social science, literature, science, and domains across the curriculum

- Vocabulary Strategies and Interactive Whiteboard Lessons to build the morphological and contextual tools students need to generate new vocabulary

- Speaking and Listening lessons with systematic instruction in collaboration skills for academic conversations

- Literacy and Language Guide with literary minilessons, leveled developmental spelling lists, and research-based word study lessons

- Integrated English Language Support to scaffold ELs during core instruction

- Standard English Learner support at point of use to help students both appreciate the language variations of their home and community and develop facility in academic, mainstream English

Effective Expression

Students express themselves through writing, speaking, digital media, and many other forms. These expressions not only reflect what students have learned, but they are also the *means* of learning.

Journeys provides students with daily opportunities to express their understandings and thinking by engaging in well-structured academic conversations about texts and topics with peers, in daily writing activities, and in collaborative projects several times per year.

Effective Expression supports include

- Collaborative Classroom Conversations and Think-Pair-Share activities to provide students with daily opportunities to express their understandings and thinking by engaging in well-structured academic conversations about texts and topics

- Language Workshop instruction to help English learners express themselves and collaborate effectively

- Extended Collaborative Projects to cultivate students' curiosity, motivation, and engagement, giving them multiple opportunities to speak informally and formally, from initial discussions through the delivery of final presentations

- Interactive Lessons in writing, speaking, and listening to provide reinforcement and practice of key skills

- *my*WriteSmart, an online tool, to support students as they write to sources, create multimedia presentations, collaborate, and share their written expressions

Content Knowledge

To make meaning of complex texts, students must develop a knowledge base that is both broad and deep.

Journeys provides students with a rich array of informational and literary texts organized around content-area domains and topics. As students compare, contrast, and synthesize ideas, they build a robust knowledge framework that captures new ideas like a net.

Content Knowledge supports include

- Informational Anchor Texts and Paired Selections focused on concepts and vocabulary that are high in interest and cross-curricular relevance

- Trade Books for in-depth exploration of topics in which students are interested

- Extend the Topic lessons to help students acquire and use topic-related domain-specific vocabulary

- Research and Media Literacy instruction to develop the skills students need to be independent learners and broadly literate thinkers

- Collaborative Projects to provide opportunities for inquiry and deep understanding of topics about which students have questions and to apply research and media literacy knowledge and skills

- FYI Site to give students the experience of finding relevant and reliable information online

- Channel One News for engaging, current media about the world in which students live

- Stream to Start Videos to kick-start interest in the unit topic through brief, high-interest videos

Foundational Skills

Student mastery of print concepts, phonological awareness, phonics and word recognition, and fluency is crucial for building literacy.

Journeys provides explicit, systematic instruction, diagnostic support, differentiated instruction, and distributed practice for the full range of foundational literacy skills with support for all students.

Foundational Skills supports include

- Phonemic Awareness and Phonics instruction that is carefully sequenced and includes built-in application and periodic review

- Decodable Readers and Blend-It Books to apply every sound-spelling correspondence in multiple contexts, building mastery

- Sound/Spelling Cards for modeling and explicit instruction in sound-spelling correspondences

- Decoding Lessons at higher grades to empower students to tackle longer words

- Fluency Lessons to build automaticity and prosody, facilitating comprehension

- HMH Decoding Power: Intensive Reading Instruction to systematically and efficiently build the strong foundational skills that many struggling students need in order to become fluent, independent readers

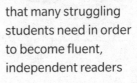

Access for each and every student

Each child requires and deserves literacy instruction that is tailored to his or her individual needs. That is why in *Journeys,* access is not an afterthought; it is the main idea, built into every component, every lesson, and every text.

Access and Equity supports include

- **Integrated Extra Support** and **English Language Support** at multiple points in every text and in every lesson

- **Text X-Rays** that break down the content and language challenges that students may encounter in every Anchor Text, to empower teacher preparation

- **Differentiated instruction** built into every lesson, as part of the core instructional routine—not as an afterthought—to give all students opportunities to engage with challenging ideas and language

- **How English Works** features in each lesson to help teachers use the texts to build linguistic awareness and skills

- **Reading Detective** and **Language Detective** features in every lesson to inspire students to read closely and to analyze language use

- **Language Workshop,** a complete, rigorous, systematic program for ELD that builds into and from the core program to enable language learners to stretch to greater proficiency in academic English

- **Write-In Reader** for practice with close reading parallel texts that help readers "ramp up" to the Anchor Text, with a Reading Detective feature every week to motivate and scaffold close reading

- **Strategic Intervention** lessons to preteach and reteach every day as needed

- **HMH Decoding Power: Intensive Reading Instruction** to systematically and efficiently build the strong foundational skills that many struggling students need in order to become fluent, independent readers

- **Intervention Assessments** to provide the data needed to inform entrances and exits in intervention and to monitor progress

Text X-Ray

Proven Results

Journeys students made significant gains across multiple studies, including an independent Gold Standard Study.

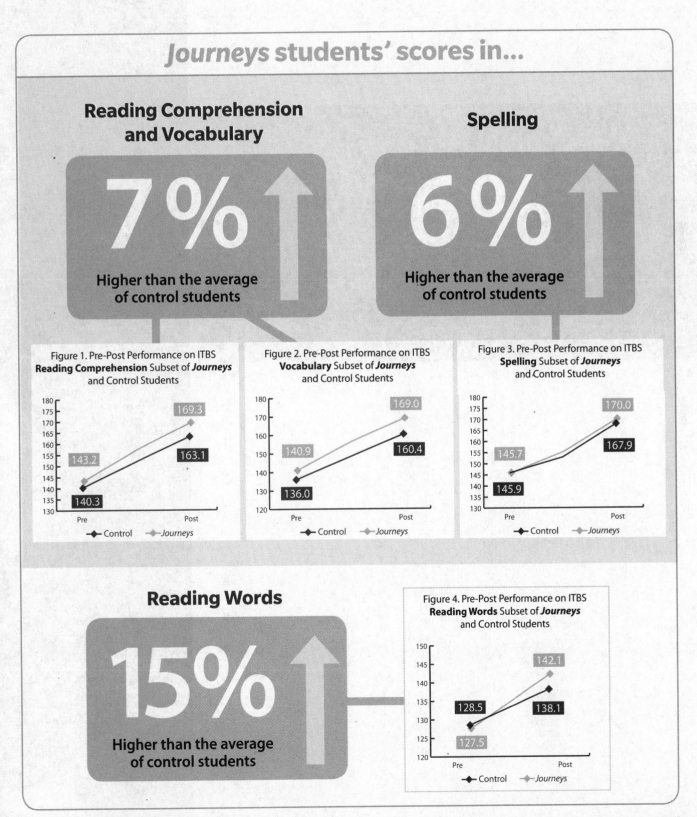

Journeys students' scores in...

Reading Comprehension and Vocabulary

7% ↑

Higher than the average of control students

Spelling

6% ↑

Higher than the average of control students

Figure 1. Pre-Post Performance on ITBS **Reading Comprehension** Subset of *Journeys* and Control Students

169.3
163.1
143.2
140.3
— Control — *Journeys*

Figure 2. Pre-Post Performance on ITBS **Vocabulary** Subset of *Journeys* and Control Students

169.0
160.4
140.9
136.0
— Control — *Journeys*

Figure 3. Pre-Post Performance on ITBS **Spelling** Subset of *Journeys* and Control Students

170.0
167.9
145.7
145.9
— Control — *Journeys*

Reading Words

15% ↑

Higher than the average of control students

Figure 4. Pre-Post Performance on ITBS **Reading Words** Subset of *Journeys* and Control Students

142.1
138.1
128.5
127.5
— Control — *Journeys*

PROGRAM FEATURES

Flexibility for Teachers, Engagement for Learners

Journeys puts an array of powerful, easy-to-use digital tools at teachers' fingertips. With a few clicks, teachers can **individualize instruction** to reach all learners, while students are fully engaged in learning challenging content through state-of-the-art digital tools.

Customizing for Combination Classrooms For multi-grade classrooms, you may want to use small-group differentiation to ensure that all students master grade-level standards. You can use *my*SmartPlanner to search for instructional resources by standard and slot them into a customized planner that meets the needs of your students.

Access all student and teacher resources from the online **Teacher Dashboard.** Use the search function to customize lessons that meet the instructional needs of all your students.

The **Student Dashboard** gives learners access to a wealth of resources, including the Student eBook, *my*WriteSmart, interactive digital lessons, and up-to-date informational articles related to unit themes and topics.

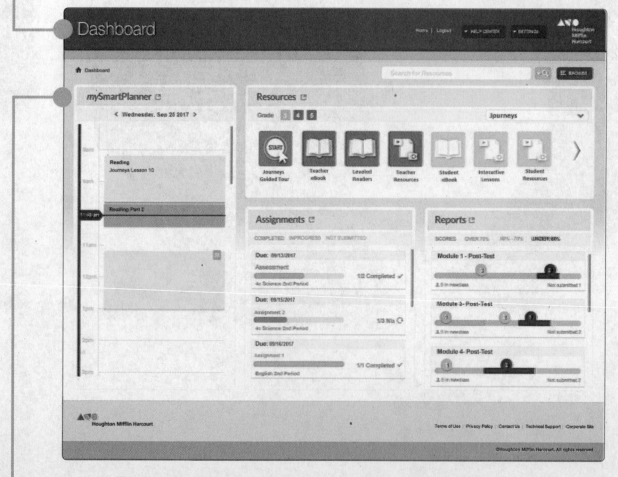

Use ***my*SmartPlanner** to plan your entire daily, weekly, monthly, or yearly schedule and easily populate lesson plans for the year. You can also modify the plans and save them from year to year.

HMHPLAYER
Making 1:1 Learning a Reality

Customize
Access offline
Sync-able
Import Media
Collaborate

**Anytime,
Anywhere**

The **HMH Player**™ provides students and teachers with anytime/anywhere access to *Journeys*.

- Users can access key components of the program offline, then sync work when they return online.

- Teachers can integrate their own lessons along with open-source content, images, and videos to customize or create new lessons.

- Teachers and students can collaborate with one another in an easy and engaging way.

Flexibility for Teachers, Engagement for Learners

Intuitive digital tools in the Student and Teacher's Edition eBooks provide instructional support and make learning dynamic and interactive.

Teacher's Edition eBooks provide point-of-use access to unit- and lesson-specific instructional materials.

Links to online features from **Student eBook** Unit Openers make instruction relevant to student interests.

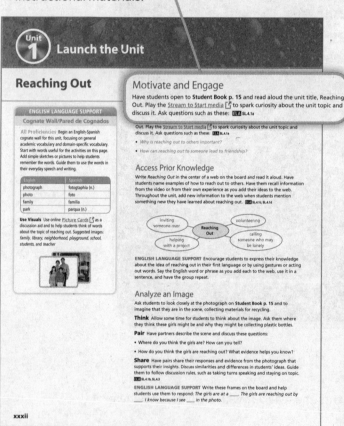

Stream to Start Videos introduce the topic of the unit in a format that will engage diverse learners. They also encourage meaningful peer discussions and build background for lessons in the unit.

Use the award-winning daily news program **Channel One News** to spark conversations on current events and foster critical thinking skills.

Engage students with real-world connections through the **FYI site.** *FYI* provides contemporary informational texts and media, motivating visuals, and suggested trade book titles for each *Journeys* unit topic.

Student Book Content

Journeys delivers instruction through authentic, award-winning texts students love to read. Literary and informational selections, many of them exemplar texts, provide rich and engaging reading experiences for all learners.

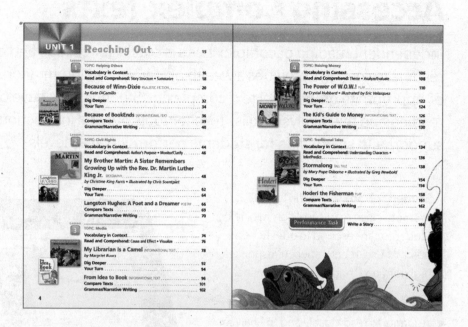

Interactive Lessons

Student-directed digital lessons in writing and listening and speaking extend and enrich instruction in an engaging way.

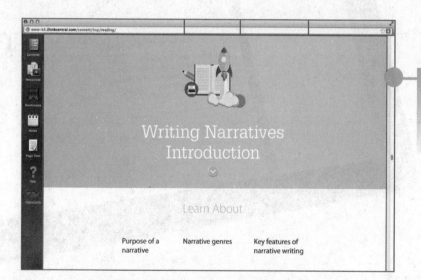

Interactive Whiteboard Lessons

Hands-on lessons in vocabulary strategies, grammar, text analysis, and writing and research skills engage students in the learning process.

Accessing Complex Texts

Independent reading of complex texts is crucial for college and career readiness. *Journeys* provides a wealth of literary and informational texts of appropriate grade-level text complexity. Student tools develop close reading and text analysis skills; teacher tools provide instructional support and scaffolding for students performing at all levels.

Student eBooks provide tools that promote close reading of complex texts. Students can respond to questions at point-of-use, record spoken responses, highlight text, and take notes online.

"Be a Reading Detective" inspires students to read closely and to analyze the use of language.

myNotebook allows students to collect and organize their notes in preparation for writing and discussions.

Students can use ***myWordList*** to tag vocabulary terms and unfamiliar words as they read and collect them in *my*Notebook, building their own personal word list.

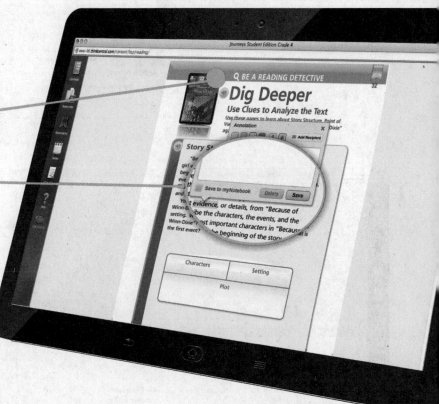

Reader's Notebook provides prompts and questions for text analysis, as well as practice with reading comprehension, writing, and language skills.

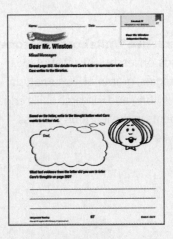

Reading Adventures Magazines include motivating texts and activities on a variety of engaging topics for students in Grades 3-5.

Text Complexity Rubrics for each selection save valuable time by helping teachers gauge both quantitative and qualitative text complexity at a glance. **Text X-Rays** break down the key ideas in the text and provide a way to make challenging concepts comprehensible to all students.

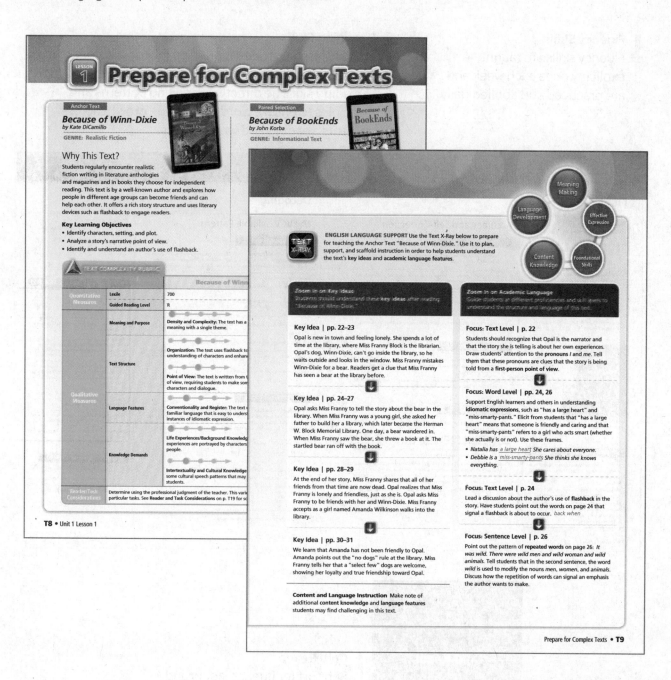

For Professional
Development resources, go to
www.thinkcentral.com.

Foundational Skills
Fluency and Decoding

Fluency Skills
Fluency skills are taught explicitly once each week and are practiced and applied daily.

Decoding Skills
In every lesson, students practice recognizing decoding elements and applying them to reading fluency practice. Decoding skills tie directly to spelling patterns and principles to ensure word knowledge growth across students' reading and writing tasks.

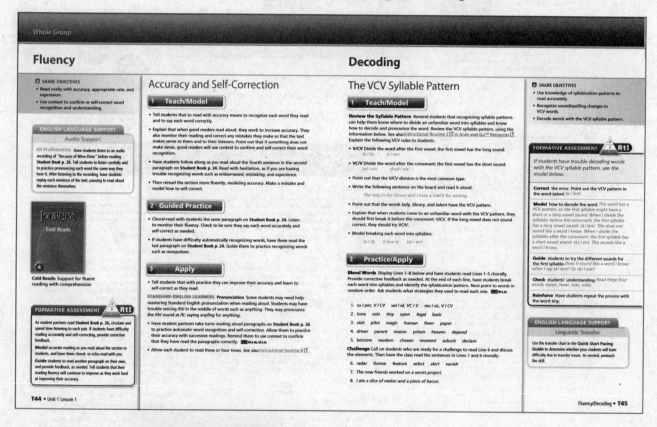

Whole Group

Fluency

SHARE OBJECTIVES
- Read orally with accuracy, appropriate rate, and expression.
- Use context to confirm or self-correct word recognition and understanding.

ENGLISH LANGUAGE SUPPORT
Audio Support

All Proficiencies Have students listen to an audio recording of "Because of Winn-Dixie" before reading **Student Book p. 26**. Tell students to listen carefully and to practice pronouncing each word the same way they hear it. After listening to the recording, have students replay each sentence of the text, pausing to read aloud the sentence themselves.

Cold Reads: Support for fluent reading with comprehension

Accuracy and Self-Correction

1 Teach/Model
- Tell students that to read with accuracy means to recognize each word they read and to say each word correctly.
- Explain that when good readers read aloud, they work to increase accuracy. They also monitor their reading and correct any mistakes they make so that the text makes sense to them and to their listeners. Point out that if something does not make sense, good readers will use context to confirm and self-correct their word recognition.
- Have students follow along as you read aloud the fourth sentence in the second paragraph on **Student Book p. 24**. Read with hesitation, as if you are having trouble recognizing words such as *embarrassed, mistaking,* and *experience.*
- Then reread the section more fluently, modeling accuracy. Make a mistake and model how to self-correct.

2 Guided Practice
- Choral-read with students the same paragraph on **Student Book p. 24**. Listen to monitor their fluency. Check to be sure they say each word accurately and self-correct as needed.
- If students have difficulty automatically recognizing words, have them read the last paragraph on **Student Book p. 24**. Guide them to practice recognizing words such as *mosquitoes.*

3 Apply
- Tell students that with practice they can improve their accuracy and learn to self-correct as they read.

STANDARD ENGLISH LEARNERS Pronunciation Some students may need help mastering Standard English pronunciation when reading aloud. Students may have trouble voicing /th/ in the middle of words such as *anything.* They may pronounce the /th/ sound as /t/, saying *anyting* for *anything.*
- Have student partners take turns reading aloud paragraphs on **Student Book p. 26** to practice automatic word recognition and self-correction. Allow them to practice their accuracy with successive readings. Remind them to use context to confirm that they have read the paragraphs correctly.
- Allow each student to read three or four times. See also Instructional Routine 8.

FORMATIVE ASSESSMENT RtI

As student partners read **Student Book p. 26**, circulate and spend time listening to each pair. If students have difficulty reading accurately and self-correcting, provide corrective feedback.

Model accurate reading as you read aloud the section to students, and have them choral- or echo-read with you.

Guide students to read another paragraph on their own, and provide feedback, as needed. Tell students that their reading fluency will continue to improve as they work hard at improving their accuracy.

T44 • Unit 1 Lesson 1

Decoding

The VCV Syllable Pattern

1 Teach/Model

Review the Syllable Pattern Remind students that recognizing syllable patterns can help them know where to divide an unfamiliar word into syllables and know how to decode and pronounce the word. Review the VCV syllable pattern, using the information below. See also Instructional Routine 2 in Grab-and-Go™ Resources. Explain the following VCV rules to students:
- **V/CV** Divide the word after the first vowel; the first vowel has the long sound:
  la / dy   e / ven
- **VC/V** Divide the word after the consonant; the first vowel has the short sound:
  tal / ent   shad / ow
- Point out that the V/CV division is the most common type.
- Write the following sentence on the board and read it aloud:
  The lady in the library said I have a talent for writing.
- Point out that the words *lady, library,* and *talent* have the VCV pattern.
- Explain that when students come to an unfamiliar word with the VCV pattern, they should first break it before the consonant: V/CV. If the long vowel does not sound correct, they should try VC/V.
- Model breaking each word into syllables:
  la / dy   li-bra-ry   tal / ent

2 Practice/Apply

Blend Words Display Lines 1–8 below and have students read Lines 1–5 chorally. Provide corrective feedback as needed. At the end of each line, have students break each word into syllables and identify the syllabication pattern. Next point to words in random order. Ask students what strategies they used to read each one.

1. su / per, V / CV   val / id, VC / V   mu / sic, V / CV
2. tuna   solo   tiny   open   legal   basic
3. visit   pilot   magic   human   fever   paper
4. driver   parent   reason   prison   heaven   depend
5. become   modern   chosen   moment   suburb   declare

Challenge Call on students who are ready for a challenge to read Line 6 and discuss the elements. Then have the class read the sentences in Lines 7 and 8 chorally.

6. radar   license   feature   select   alert   vanish
7. The new friends worked on a secret project.
8. I ate a slice of melon and a piece of bacon.

SHARE OBJECTIVES
- Use knowledge of syllabication patterns to read accurately.
- Recognize sound/spelling changes in VCV words.
- Decode words with the VCV syllable pattern.

FORMATIVE ASSESSMENT RtI

If students have trouble decoding words with the VCV syllable pattern, use the model below.

Correct the error. Point out the VCV pattern in the word *talent.* tal / ent

Model how to decode the word. This word has a VCV pattern, so the first syllable might have a short or a long vowel sound. When I divide the syllables before the consonant, the first syllable has a long vowel sound: tā / lent. This does not sound like a word I know. When I divide the syllables after the consonant, the first syllable has a short vowel sound: tă l / ent. This sounds like a word I know.

Guide students to try the different sounds for the first syllable. Does it sound like a word I know when I say tā / lent? Or tă l / ent?

Check students' understanding. Read these four words: seven, fever, solo, solid.

Reinforce Have students repeat the process with the word tiny.

ENGLISH LANGUAGE SUPPORT
Linguistic Transfer

Use the transfer chart in the Quick Start Pacing Guide to determine whether your students will have difficulty due to transfer issues. As needed, preteach the skill.

Fluency/Decoding • T45

Cold Reads
Support for fluent reading and for assessing comprehension

Intensive Intervention

HMH Decoding Power: Intensive Reading Instruction provides targeted intervention for students needing intensive support in one or more of the key foundational reading skills.

HMH Decoding Power provides **explicit, sequential,** and **systematic instruction,** as well as practice and review in the critical areas of print concepts:

- Letter Knowledge
- Phonological Awareness
- Phonemic Awareness
- Phonics
- Word Recognition
- Fluency

Instruction at multiple grade levels enables teachers to gradually bring struggling students up to grade level.

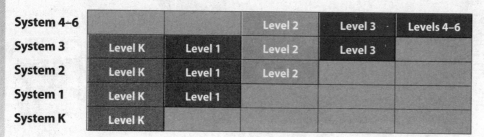

System 4–6			Level 2	Level 3	Levels 4–6
System 3	Level K	Level 1	Level 2	Level 3	
System 2	Level K	Level 1	Level 2		
System 1	Level K	Level 1			
System K	Level K				

The HMH K-12 intervention solution also includes **System 44** (Grades 3-12+) and **READ 180** (Grades 4-12+), online intervention programs designed to address Tier 2 and Tier 3 students. More information about these products is available online.

For Professional Development resources, go to www.thinkcentral.com.

Language
Building Word Knowledge

Journeys provides comprehensive vocabulary instruction in the context of high-quality texts. Students deepen their word knowledge with strategies taught and reinforced through an array of print and online resources.

Academic and Domain Vocabulary

Weekly lessons on academic and domain-specific vocabulary tied to the Anchor Texts help students build their vocabulary knowledge.

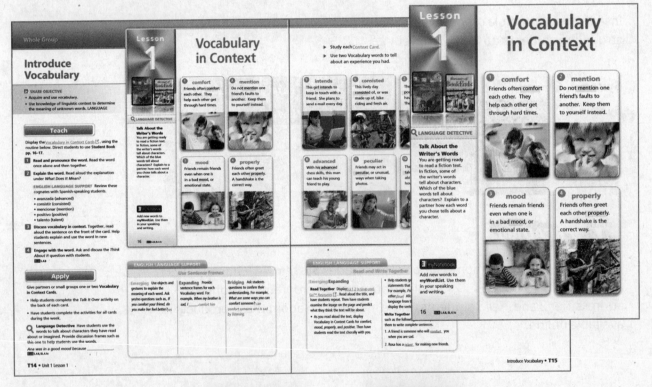

Vocabulary in Context Cards

Students deepen their vocabulary knowledge by engaging with the photograph, context sentence, and definition for each Target Vocabulary word.

The **Vocabulary Reader** for each lesson provides additional practice with the vocabulary introduced in the Anchor Text.

Vocabulary Strategies lessons give students the morphological and contextual tools they need to determine and confirm the meanings of unfamiliar words and to generate new vocabulary.

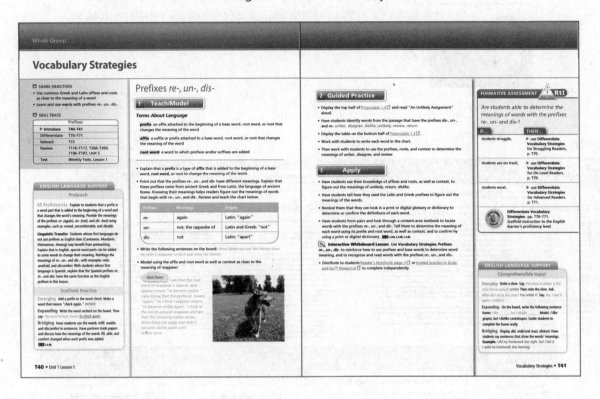

Interactive Whiteboard Lessons provide engaging, hands-on weekly practice and reinforcement in language skills.

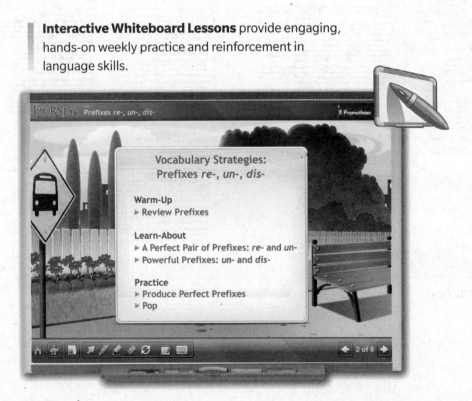

Language

Literacy and Language Guide includes weekly lesson plans for word study, reading, and writing. A planning page for each lesson provides a clear pathway through each week of instruction and seamlessly connects the parts of the plan.

Spelling/Phonics

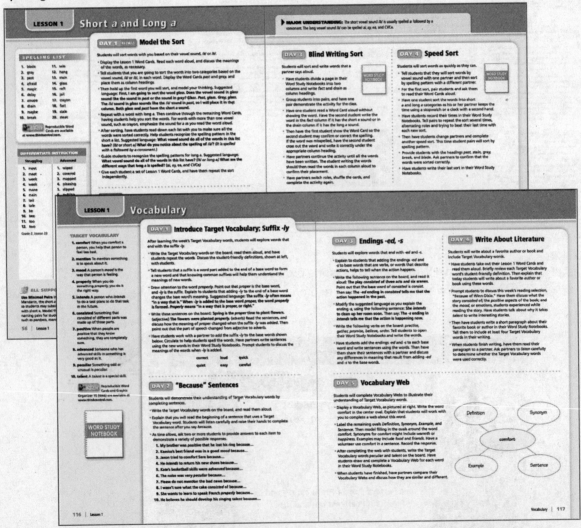

Vocabulary

Language
Learning and Applying Grammar

Instructional strategies in *Journeys* help all learners gain control over conventions of Standard English grammar, usage, and mechanics so they can understand content and express ideas at their grade level.

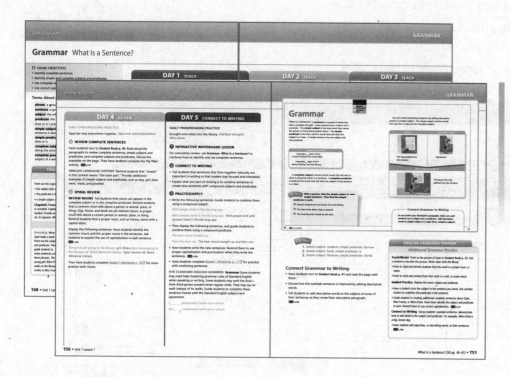

Core grammar instruction connected to writing develops students' abilities to convey meaning effectively using conventional grammatical structures.

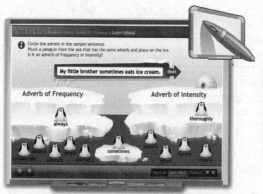

Interactive Whiteboard Lessons provide weekly practice and reinforcement in grammar skills.

GrammarSnap Videos demonstrate grammar concepts through short, high-energy videos.

The **Multimedia Grammar Glossary** reinforces grammar skills with fun, interactive activities, organized alphabetically for easy reference.

For Professional Development resources, go to www.thinkcentral.com.

Writing

Journeys provides comprehensive instruction and support for a full range of student writing tasks. Students gain weekly practice in Writing to Sources, as well as in Narrative, Informative, and Opinion Writing through the Writing Process.

Writing Instruction

- Students focus on one mode of writing across each unit, giving them a depth of understanding as they complete a variety of tasks.

- During the last two weeks of a unit, students follow the steps of the writing process through publishing.

- Integrated ELD support is provided in the Teacher's Edition.

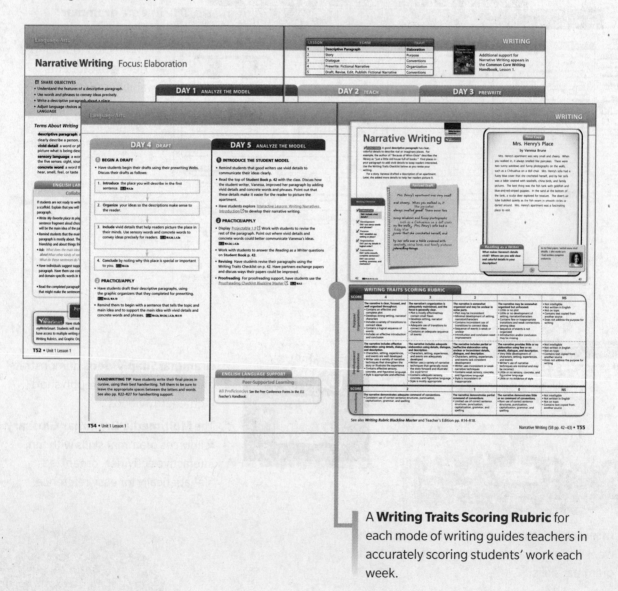

A **Writing Traits Scoring Rubric** for each mode of writing guides teachers in accurately scoring students' work each week.

Performance Tasks in each unit of the Student Book provide step-by-step guidance in analyzing and synthesizing complex texts before writing a critical response.

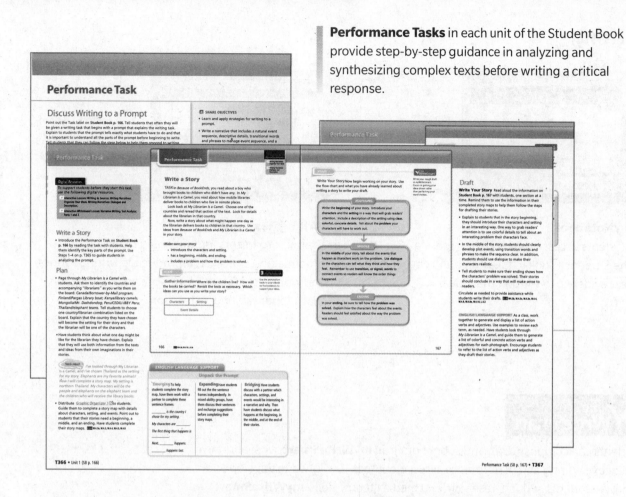

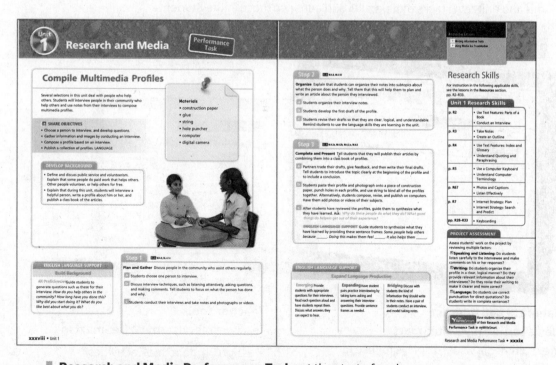

Research and Media Performance Tasks at the start of each unit in the Teacher's Edition provide students with multiple opportunities to develop and publish collaborative research projects of varying lengths.

Writing

*my*Notebook

Students access this annotation tool via the Student eBook to take notes and cite text evidence to support their ideas.

Writing Resources

Graphic organizers, proofreading marks, a proofreading checklist, reproducible writing rubrics, and writing conference forms are among the tools that support writing instruction.

Students can compose, edit, and submit drafts in ***myWriteSmart***, a collaborative, interactive writing and performance assessment tool. Designed to develop and improve students' writing, research, and media literacy skills, ***myWriteSmart*** includes lesson- and unit-level tasks that parallel and enhance those in the Student Book and Teacher's Edition.

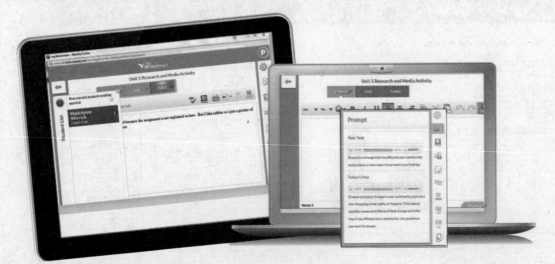

Collaborate and Interact

Students can use ***myWriteSmart*** to create multimedia visual displays for use in presentations.

Students collaborate by sharing their work with other students and their teacher, who can give instant online feedback.

Teacher Tools

Teachers may use ***myWriteSmart*** to

- assign Student Book activities
- track student work
- comment on student writing
- access rubrics
- link to additional tools and resources

Interactive Lessons give students the opportunity for digital, independent practice in critical writing skills.

- Writing to Sources
- Writing Narratives
- Writing Opinions
- Writing Informative Texts
- Writing as a Process
- Producing and Publishing with Technology

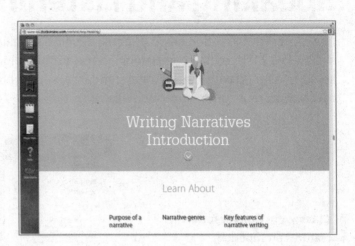

Interactive Whiteboard Lessons supplement print instruction in opinion, informative, and narrative writing modes. Each lesson reviews taught skills, and provides teacher-led instruction, guided practice, and independent application opportunities for whole-class engagement.

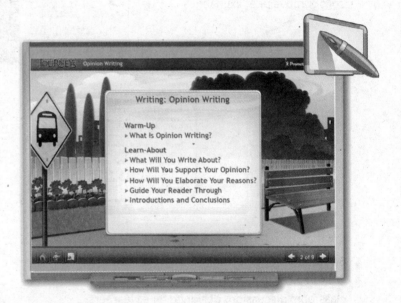

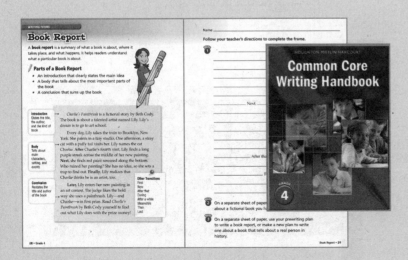

Common Core Writing Handbook complements the writing instruction in *Journeys*. It provides students with a model for each form, scaffolded practice, and a handbook resource. The Teacher's Guide provides minilessons for every handbook topic.

For Professional Development resources, go to www.thinkcentral.com.

Speaking and Listening

Journeys core instruction helps students develop speaking and listening skills —key 21st-century competencies. In addition, digital Interactive Lessons, aligned with instructional standards, support the acquisition of these important communication skills.

Classroom Conversation features prompt rich, collaborative peer exchanges.

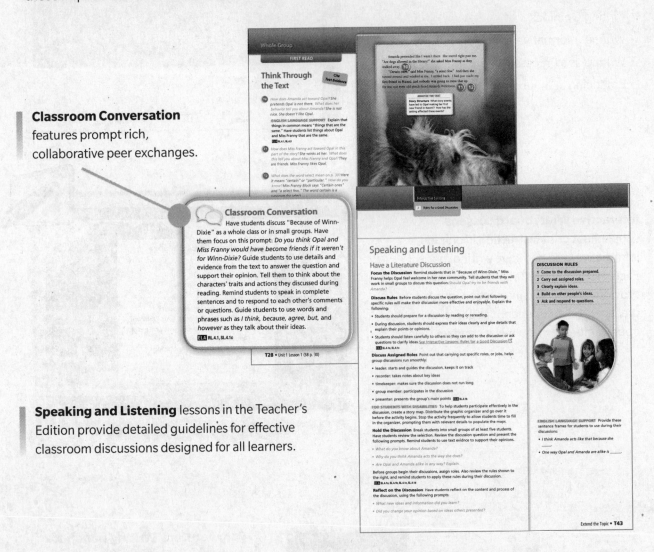

Speaking and Listening lessons in the Teacher's Edition provide detailed guidelines for effective classroom discussions designed for all learners.

Interactive Lessons
Student-directed digital lessons in listening and speaking extend and enrich instruction in an engaging way.

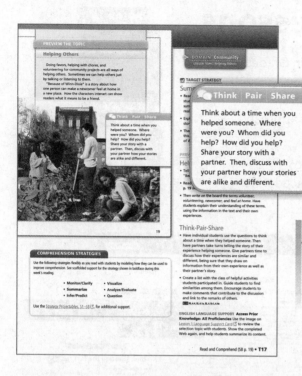

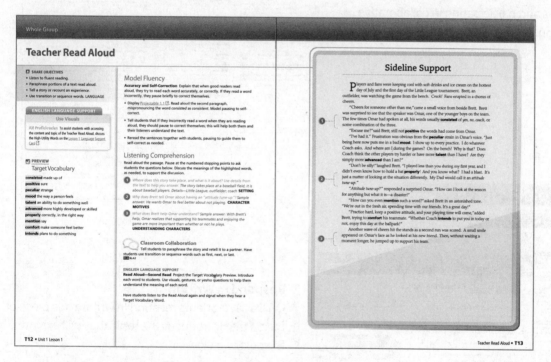

Think/Pair/Share activities are ideal for engaging all students in academic conversations.

Think/Write/Pair/Share activities provide a variation in which students write their ideas before collaborating with a partner.

Teacher Read Alouds at the start of each lesson promote listening comprehension and provide models of fluent reading.

Extended Reading Lessons

Read Trade Books Three times per year, students in Grades 1-5 spend up to two weeks with a full-length trade book. Drawing on their close-reading experiences with shorter literary and informational texts each week, students approach these extended texts in the same way.

A Text X-Ray for each trade book provides scaffolding support for key text features such as text structure, academic vocabulary, and figurative language.

Analyze Complex Texts

After reading and thinking through each text segment in a first read, students dig deeper to analyze it in a second read, answering critical questions and participating in collaborative discussion.

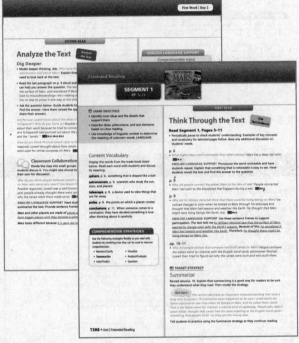

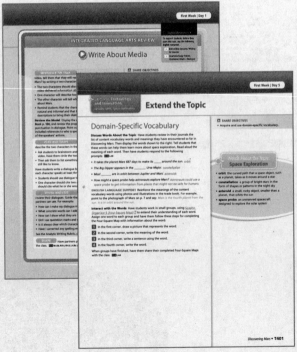

Respond in Writing

On Day 1, students respond in writing to a piece of media that introduces the topic they will explore over the next two weeks.

Students write a daily analytical response to their reading, incorporating acquired language arts skills, as appropriate to the task.

Extend the Topic

Students explore and discuss domain-specific vocabulary related to the topic, deepening their understanding of words and concepts.

Collaborate on Projects

Throughout the two weeks, students work collaboratively on a meaningful project tied to the topic. Students develop and build 21st-century skills, applying reading, writing, speaking, listening, research, and technology skills in the process.

The project is initiated with a launch, followed by discussion and preparation, during which the project is developed. Students present their projects to an audience, are assessed with a project rubric, celebrate, and, finally, reflect on the outcome of this interactive and engaging learning experience.

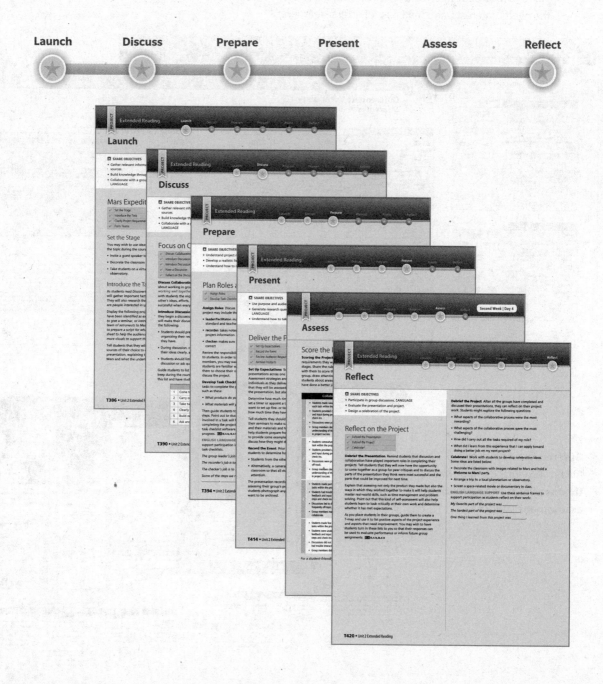

Access and Equity
Unlocking the Potential of All Students

The array of dynamic digital tools in *Journeys* provides **universal access**, enabling diverse learners at all levels to access grade-level content.

Differentiated Instruction

Journeys provides evidence-based instructional approaches to address the needs, interests, and readiness of diverse learners.

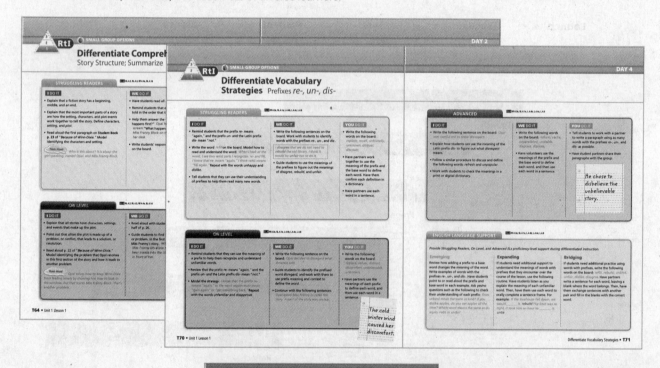

Differentiation in every Anchor Text includes **just-in-time scaffolds** and **formative assessment support.**

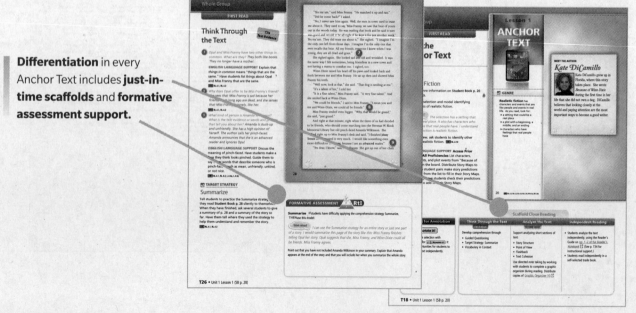

Flexible Grouping

Journeys provides a wealth of **whole-class** and **small-group resources** that provide all students the opportunity to engage with complex text and to interact with peers.

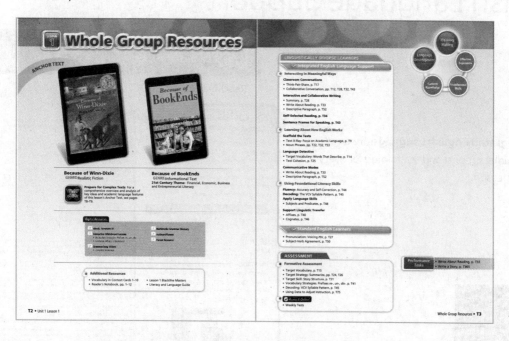

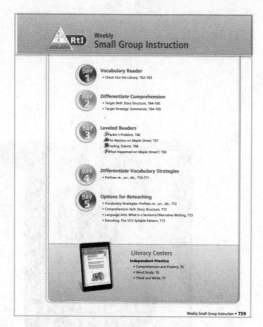

Support for **Small-Group Instruction** includes Leveled Reader lesson plans, as well as options for reteaching key skills.

Write-In Readers are consumable worktexts that preteach and reteach weekly skills and vocabulary.

- As **targeted intervention,** the Write-In Readers encourage struggling students to make the text their own by annotating it and taking notes. This helps prepare them for success with the week's Anchor Text.

- Students develop **close reading** habits that build their ability to analyze and synthesize complex texts independently.

- **Weekly Reading Detective** features provide motivation and step-by-step scaffolding to help students "ramp-up" to the Anchor Text.

Access and Equity
English Language Support

Integrated English Language instruction provides support and scaffolding for every core lesson.

Language Workshop provides systematic instruction to accelerate the academic language skills needed to master core program content.

Culturally Responsive Teaching

Extensive support at point of use helps teachers validate and value students' cultural and linguistic heritages. Notes also support scaffolding for different registers and dialects and for the appropriate contexts for formal and informal language.

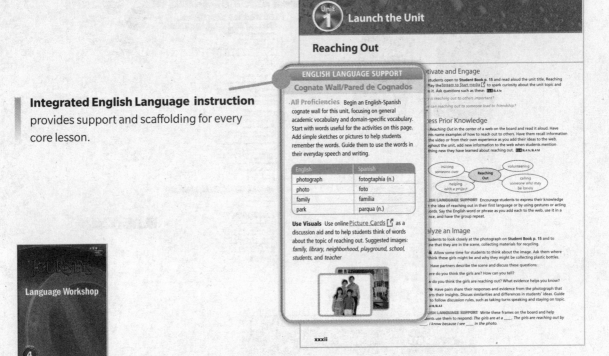

Universal Access

For visually impaired learners, *Journeys* content can be converted into **alternative assistive technology products,** such as:

- Braille
- large print
- screen reader programs

To see the range of Houghton Mifflin Harcourt products available on assistive technologies, go to the National Instructional Materials Access Center (NIMAC) **www.nimac.us/teachers.html**

Student eBook

From the eBook, students can access **full audio recordings** for each lesson.

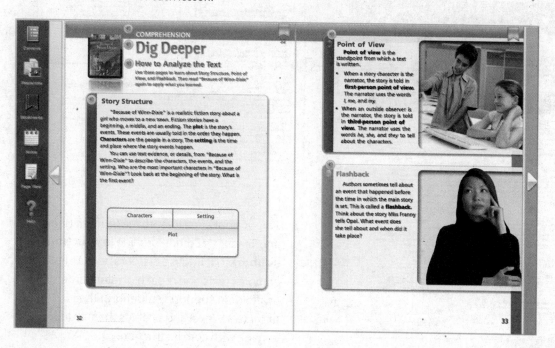

Alternative Text (Alt Text) is text provided through a screen reader that describes the content of an image in a way that not only conveys the content of the image, but also helps visually impaired users understand how the information in the image relates to the reading selection.

Closed captioning is a text alternative for audio-only elements in *Journeys* components such as Stream to Start videos, Interactive Lessons, and *Channel One News*. The captioning feature can be turned on when the audio is muted or if the user is hearing impaired.

Support for English Learners

Journeys provides research-based support to meet the needs of today's diverse classrooms. Support for learners at all stages of English proficiency ensures that every student receives a world-class 21st-century education.

Integrated Classroom Support

Support for English learners' linguistic and academic progress is built into the core program.

Text X-Rays in the Teacher's Edition identify language challenges students may encounter as they read the text. **Scaffolded instruction** helps students understand the structure and language of each text.

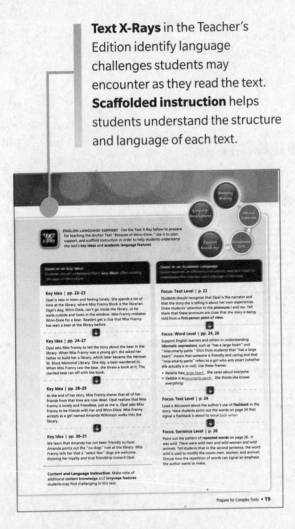

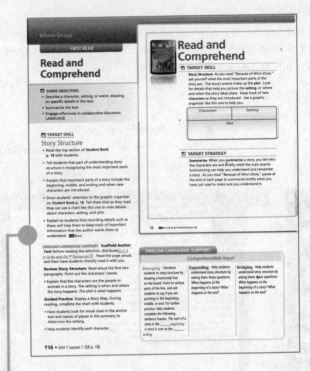

Throughout each lesson, the Student Book and Teacher's Edition provide **instructional support** that English learners need to read complex texts and meet high standards. Scaffolding supports students at their proficiency level and enables them to fully engage with core instruction.

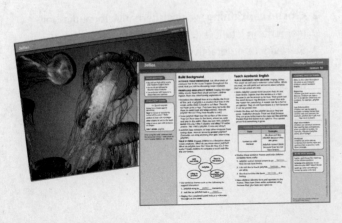

Language Support Cards
- preteach concepts
- build background and promote oral language
- develop high-utility vocabulary and academic language

Language Workshop materials support students in developing collaborative, interpretive, and productive skills, as well as in understanding how English works. English learners develop the English-language knowledge and abilities they need in order to successfully engage with core content.

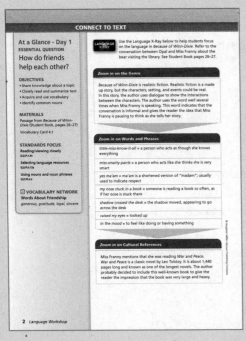

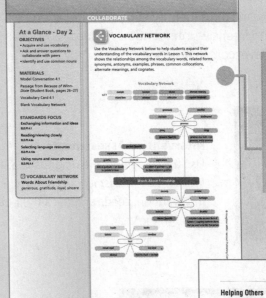

Vocabulary Network

Multiple word maps support student acquisition of vocabulary taught in each lesson.

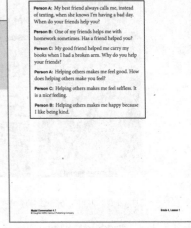

Helping Others

Person A: My best friend always calls me, instead of texting, when she knows I'm having a bad day. When do your friends help you?

Person B: One of my friends helps me with homework sometimes. Has a friend helped you?

Person C: My good friend helped me carry my books when I had a broken arm. Why do you help your friends?

Person A: Helping others makes me feel good. How does helping others make you feel?

Person C: Helping others makes me feel selfless. It is a nice feeling.

Person B: Helping others makes me happy because I like being kind.

ELL Teacher's Handbook

A comprehensive guide to EL instruction including Professional Development, Best Practices guidelines, and classroom resources

ELL Newcomer Teacher's Guide

Twelve focused, efficient lessons plus corresponding posters and videos that emphasize survival vocabulary and high-utility language functions for students who need the basics of English

For information on using native-language linguistic features to support English learners, see pages 88-95 of this Guide.

For Professional Development resources, go to www.thinkcentral.com.

Extra Support and Intervention
Building Student Confidence and Proficiency

Screening and diagnostic tools identify and prescribe appropriate support for each student. Strategic and intensive intervention resources build skills students need for success with grade-level core instruction.

Intervention Assessments
Use the screening and diagnostic assessments in *Intervention Assessments* to determine students' intervention needs and track their performance through the year.

Leveled Readers
Leveled Readers, leveled and reviewed by Irene Fountas and connected to the anchor text topic, provide practice and support for a range of student reading levels. When they read appropriately challenging texts, students develop their ability to read complex texts with increasing independence.

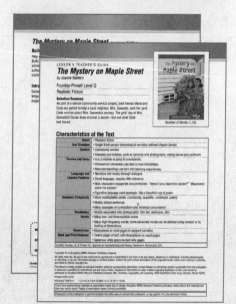

Leveled Readers Teacher's Guides
8-page lessons for each book support instruction in guided reading groups.

Student Book: Reading Detective

At the beginning of the Student Book, students are introduced to the best approach for analyzing complex texts.

Strategic Intervention: Write-In Reader

- For students reading one year below grade level, the Write-In Reader at each grade provides weekly close reading and annotation opportunities, as well as a ramp-up to each Anchor Text.

- The focus on vocabulary, comprehension, and text evidence is supported by Stop, Think, and Write interactive activities that promote learner engagement and reinforce core-program skills.

- The user-friendly format enables teachers to monitor progress quickly.

Extra Support and Intervention
Intensive Intervention

HMH Decoding Power: Intensive Reading Instruction   Provides intervention for students who need intensive support in one or more of the key foundational reading skills.

The five "systems" of Decoding Power provide explicit, sequential, and systematic instruction as well as practice and review in the critical areas of print concepts, letter knowledge, phonological awareness, phonemic awareness, phonics, word recognition, and fluency. The systems include instruction at multiple grade levels, enabling teachers to bring struggling students up to grade level.

Features

- Explicit instructional sessions that follow the steps of Teach/Model, Guided Practice, and Apply
- Reproducible practice pages at the Kindergarten through Grade 2 levels
  - Phonics Practice Pages contain decodable text (that is, at least 75 percent of the words can be decoded using known sound-spellings, while the remaining words are known high-frequency words)
  - Text passages for cumulative review and fluency practice have Lexile® measures that gradually increase
- Regularly spaced cumulative reviews, integrated with fluency practice, cement learning over time
- Formative assessment and corrective feedback notes in each session to ensure that students understand skills as they are taught
- Resources such as Alphafriends Cards, Sound/Spelling Cards, Letter Cards, High-Frequency Word Cards, and Handwriting Models

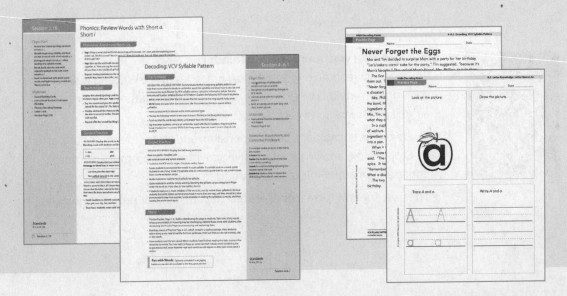

- Word games and activities for additional hands-on practice
- Point-of use language-transfer support to help English learners use what they already know while building the foundations of reading in English
- Complete alignment to, and systematic instruction for mastery of, the reading foundational skills enumerated in the Common Core State Standards
- Predecodable and decodable books available online for extra practice

The HMH K-12 intervention solution also includes **System 44** (Grades 3-12+) and **READ 180** (Grades 4-12+), online intervention programs designed to address Tier 2 and Tier 3 students. More information about these products is available online.

Intervention Assessments

- Brief enough to administer once every two weeks for students who need close monitoring
- Depending on level, assess phonological and phonemic awareness, letter-naming fluency, letter-sound fluency, word-reading fluency, and sentence- and passage-reading fluency
- Record forms that make placement, monitoring, and exit decisions automatic for teachers and understandable for family members

Components	Systems				
	K	1	2	3	4 – 6
Teacher's Guide: Instructional sessions as well as hands-on activities and other resources	√	√	√	√	√
Practice Pages: Reproducible practice pages for applying skills learned in the instructional sessions (Note that not all sessions use a Practice Page.)	√	√	√	√	√
Handwriting Models: Reproducible pages for practicing letter formation	√	√	√	√	
Alphafriends Cards: Friendly alphabet characters that help students learn letter names and sounds (Note: Audio of Alphafriends songs is available online.)	√	√	√	√	
Sound/Spelling Cards: Visual support for learning letter-sound relationships and common spelling patterns	√	√	√	√	√
Letter Cards: Set of cards containing two uppercase and four lowercase cards for each letter of the alphabet	√	√	√	√	√
High-Frequency Word Cards: Cards that feature high-frequency words and tips for decoding them	√	√	√	√	√
Intervention Assessments: Tests for checking student progress toward grade-level achievement at an appropriate pace	√	√	√	√	√
Extended Practice: Additional predecodable and decodable books available online	√	√	√	√	√

For Professional Development resources, go to www.thinkcentral.com.

Support for Advanced Learners

Journeys provides a wealth of materials for engaging and stimulating students who are performing significantly above their age group. Differentiated resources supplement and extend the curriculum, providing depth and complexity to challenge high-performing learners.

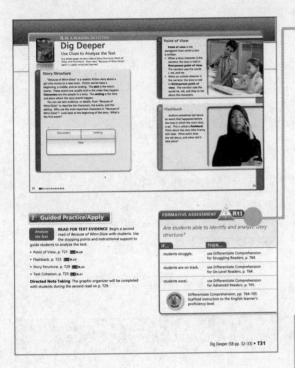

Embedded Formative Assessment

Use the Formative Assessments in the Teacher's Edition to identify learners who have mastered lesson skills.

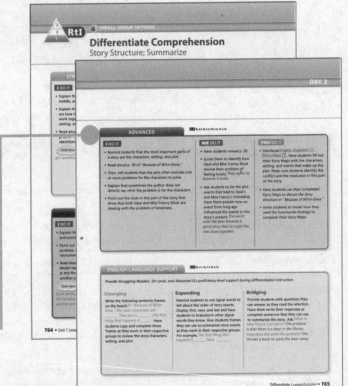

Differentiated Instruction

Use strategies and approaches in the Teacher's Edition to ensure that advanced learners are challenged and motivated.

Extended Reading Trade Books

Extended Reading Trade Books allow advanced students to work independently, while building capacity for extended close reading through systematic instructional support. Trade Books are also ideal as a basis for individual or collaborative projects.

myWriteSmart

Advanced learners can use *my*WriteSmart to improve their 21st-century digital communication and collaboration skills. They can create research reports, multimedia presentations, and other writing and media products either individually or in collaboration with other students.

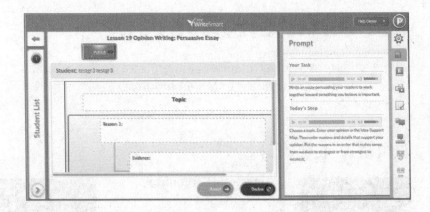

Performance Assessment and Practice

Performance Tasks provide advanced students with the opportunity to excel by responding analytically to synthesize the ideas in complex texts.

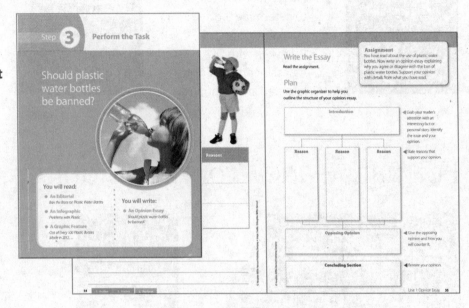

HMH Readers App

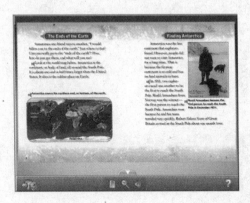

HMH Readers App gives students anytime/anywhere access to Leveled Readers. Students can work at their own pace or as part of a collaborative group.

Leveled Readers

Advanced Leveled Readers provide opportunities for high-performing students to engage with appropriately challenging text and content.

For Professional Development resources, go to www.thinkcentral.com.

Assessment System

Journeys features a powerful suite of integrated assessments that track student data and analyze student progress.

Entry Level

Universal Screening
- Use the Screening Assessments in *Intervention Assessments* to determine the need for intervention.
- Follow up with Diagnostic Assessments to inform targeted intervention

Language Workshop Assessment Handbook
- Measure progress of English learners across proficiency levels

Formative and Progress Monitoring

Benchmark and Unit Tests
- Monitor progress in comprehension of complex texts and opinion, informative, and narrative writing
- Prepare students for high-stakes assessments with constructed-response Performance Tasks

Common Core Practice and Assessment App (Android and iOS)
- Provides ongoing, low-pressure practice with high-stakes test item types
- Corrective feedback promotes growth
- Sends data in real time to teachers

Standards-Based Assessment Resource
- Assessments and Performance Tasks monitor student progress toward high-stakes tests
- Rigorous tasks and questions, complex text passages, and technology-enhanced item formats (online only) provide valuable student practice

Intervention Assessments
- Progress-Monitoring Assessments measure progress of students receiving intervention instruction

Performance Assessment
- Performance Tasks include guided instruction and practice

Summative

CONTINUUM ASSESSMENTS

- The Continuum Assessment System Benchmark Assessments provide valid and reliable measures of student growth over time
- Item difficulty adapts to each student
- Technology-enhanced item formats reflect and measure 21st-century skills and concepts
- Built to Common Core State Standards

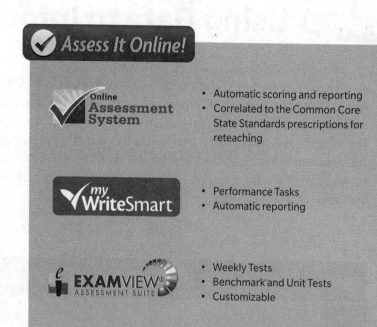

Assess It Online!

Online Assessment System
- Automatic scoring and reporting
- Correlated to the Common Core State Standards prescriptions for reteaching

myWriteSmart
- Performance Tasks
- Automatic reporting

EXAMVIEW® ASSESSMENT SUITE
- Weekly Tests
- Benchmark and Unit Tests
- Customizable

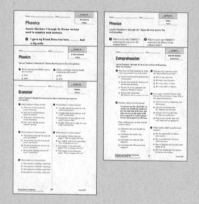

Weekly Tests

- Assess the Common Core State Standards taught in each lesson
- Monitor progress on key skills and vocabulary
- Use oral and written constructed responses to assess language and comprehension skills

Running Records

- Record a student's key reading behaviors and understanding
- Also available for each Leveled Reader

Cold Reads

- Correlated to the Common Core State Standards
- Comprehension questions and written responses
- Fluency and comprehension measured at increasing Lexiles®

Using Data to Inform Instruction

At the beginning of the school year, use the Screening Assessment in **Intervention Assessments** to screen all students for reading difficulties. Use the Diagnostic Assessment to follow up with students who demonstrated reading difficulties on the Screening Assessment. Then follow the recommendations in **Intervention Assessments** to determine the best intervention path for each identified student. Instruction that addresses individual needs and skills ensures educational access and equity for all students.

Tier I Core Instruction

Using Data

Research-Based Core Instruction includes English Language Development scaffolds integrated throughout. Use **embedded supports and scaffolds** to reach all learners.

Differentiate instruction to meet each learner's needs.

Use **Options for Reteaching** to ensure that all students receive the instruction they need to meet the key objectives of each lesson.

Use **Language Workshop** to help English learners quickly increase their level of English proficiency.

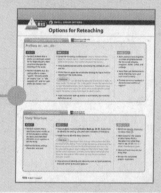

Gathering Data

Use embedded **Formative Assessment** during core instruction to provide immediate feedback at point of use.

Weekly Tests in Grab-and-Go™ at the end of each lesson can be used to check students' progress with the major skills in each lesson.

Use the Tools for Formative Assessment in the **Language Workshop Assessment Handbook** during each lesson to monitor students' English proficiency levels.

Administer the **Benchmark and Unit Tests** at the end of each Unit to determine students' overall progress with the Common Core State Standards.

Use the assessments in the **Standards-Based Assessment Resource** to monitor progress in acquiring proficiency with close reading and analytic responding. The tests can also help gauge student readiness for high-stakes assessments and performance tasks.

Tiers and Components

The "tiers" of a multi-tiered system refer to the amount of support that a student requires. How the various intervention components should be used with each student should be determined by the student's specific needs. For example, some students in "Tier II" may benefit from instruction in foundational skills, using **HMH Decoding Power: Intensive Reading Instruction**, if the data indicate a need for growth in this area.

Tips for Intervention Success

- Consider multiple measures of student performance in accordance with your school's plan for Response to Intervention.
- Provide all students with opportunities to engage with complex text and to interact with peers.
- Keep family members informed and involved.

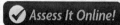

✓ Assess It Online!

- Online Tests with automatic scoring and reporting
- Correlated to Common Core State Standards
- Prescriptions for reteaching to meet Common Core State Standards
- Student Profile System to track student growth
- Reports for teacher, administrators, and parents

Tier II Strategic Intervention

Tier III Intensive Intervention

Write-In Reader

Based on the results of the Screening and Diagnostic Assessments, provide students with strategic intervention using the **Write-In Reader** and the Intervention lesson pages in the Teacher's Edition.

HMH Decoding Power: Intensive Reading Instruction K, 1, 2, 3, and 4-6

Based on the results of the Screening and Diagnostic Assessments, provide students with targeted, intensive intervention using **HMH Decoding Power: Intensive Reading Instruction.**

Intervention Assessments: Progress-Monitoring Assessments

In addition to Tier I assessments, use the Progress-Monitoring Assessments in **Intervention Assessments** to gauge student progress towards exit from the strategic intervention plan.

Intervention Assessments: Progress-Monitoring Assessments

In addition to Tier I assessments, use the Progress-Monitoring Assessments in **Intervention Assessments** to gauge student progress towards exit from the intensive intervention plan.

Preparing for Performance Assessments

Journeys assessment materials offer tools and practice opportunities to prepare students for standards-based assessments.

Performance Tasks, a centerpiece of many high-stakes assessments, typically have students closely read one or more complex texts and respond to questions about the texts in a variety of item formats. *Journeys* provides numerous opportunities for students to become experienced with Performance Tasks, while also providing teachers with the feedback they need to ensure students can master these challenging activities. *Journeys* Performance Tasks:

- align with the **text complexity requirements** of the Common Core State Standards
- include questions about individual texts as well as questions that require **comparison, contrast,** and **synthesis** across multiple texts
- require that students use **text evidence** when **writing in response to texts**

The **Benchmark and Unit Tests** are a **comprehensive assessment** of the Common Core State Standards, given at the end of each unit. **Performance Tasks** that follow each Benchmark or Unit Test use **text-embedded questions** to assess students' ability to closely read one or more complex texts and provide text-based evidence in response to questions. The items are in **Constructed Response** format, requiring students to write effectively when analyzing text. The Benchmark and Unit Tests Teacher Edition includes sample answers for quick and easy scoring of the Performance Tasks.

The **Standards-Based Assessment Resource** includes Assessments and **Performance Tasks** that align with the content in *Journeys* and give students practice with the kinds of items they will encounter on high-stakes tests. Rigorous tasks and questions, complex text, and technology-enhanced item formats (online only) prepare students for success on standards-based assessments.

The interactive online writing and performance assessment program **myWriteSmart** prepares students for the writing required by the Common Core State Standards. Lesson- and unit-level tasks parallel and enhance those in the Student Book and Teacher's Edition.

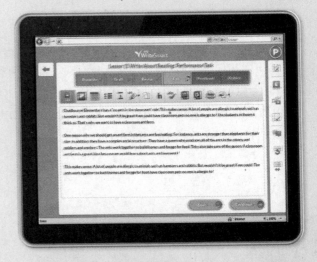

Lesson-Level Support

*my*WriteSmart supports each lesson's **Performance Tasks,** including **Write About Reading,** the **Narrative, Information,** and **Opinion Writing** tasks, and a **Research and Media Literacy** activity. With *my*WriteSmart, students may call up Student Book texts to cite evidence, access multiple resources for research and for writing improvement, practice their keyboarding skills, collaborate with classmates, interact with the teacher, and publish their work in a digital portfolio.

Unit-Level Support

At the unit level, *my*WriteSmart provides support for the **Research and Media Performance Task,** an extended **collaborative project,** and allows students to create **multimedia presentations** appropriate to the task. It also includes tools and support for **the end-of-unit Performance Task**.

Performance Assessment provides students with opportunities to practice the tasks they will encounter on high-stakes assessments. Each **Performance Task** is broken down into three parts: analyze the model, practice the task, and perform the task. This routine can be replicated for any performance task students face on high-stakes assessments. The **Performance Assessment Teacher's Guide** provides an introduction to Performance Assessments, Close Reading of Complex Texts, Writing from Sources (Opinion, Response to Literature, Research Simulation), and Performance Assessment Practice and Answer Key.

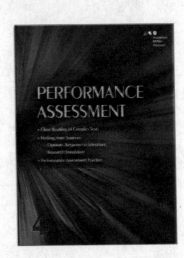

The **Continuum Assessment System Benchmark Assessments** are a valid and reliable way to track student growth within and across years. These adaptive assessments, which include technology-enhanced item formats, can be used to identify student strengths or needs, inform instruction, and predict high-stakes test performance.

Technology Rotations in Your Classroom:
A Blended Learning Model

Blended Learning is . . .

A combination of face-to-face and online engagement that ensures optimal instruction and practice for every learning event. Every resource in *Journeys* is available in both offline and online formats, enabling teachers to maximize learning across all media, at their discretion.

Online learning provides solutions to many teaching challenges

- Personalizing learning

- Engaging students at higher depth-of-knowledge levels

- Aligning to rigorous performance standards

- Differentiating instruction

- Assessing and reporting progress

- Using data efficiently to inform instruction

Types of Rotations*

Station	Within classroom, students rotate among a variety of online and offline learning stations.
Individual	Each student has an individual playlist to follow when rotating through stations.
Lab	Students rotate to computer labs for assessment and online learning stations, while using the classroom for teacher-led instruction.
Flipped	Students receive core instruction online at home (often through teacher-created videos), and in-class time is reserved for in-class practice/application, teacher coaching, and projects.

* Clayton Christensen Institute for Disruptive Innovation

Using *Journeys* in a Blended Environment

Whole Class	Small Groups
Device-friendly Teacher's Editions free teachers to engage students, model specific objectives, and rotate around the class to guide student practice. Prompts in the Teacher's Edition cue the teacher to have students annotate the text at critical complexity points, and use their ebooks to respond to questions.	**Resources for Intervention** tie back to core instruction, ensuring students across the learning spectrum access to grade-level content. • *HMH Decoding Power: Intensive Reading Instruction* delivers intensive instruction to readers who are performing at least one year below grade level. • *Write-In-Readers* are consumable worktexts that preteach and reteach weekly core skills and vocabulary to help struggling readers access classroom instruction. • Differentiated instruction accompanies each lesson in the Teacher's Edition, which also provides scaffolded support for students at a variety of levels.
Interactive Whiteboard Lessons engage students in foundational and language skills practice.	**Language Workshop** provides English learners at all proficiency levels with the academic and domain-specific language instruction they need for accessing and mastering core lessons.
Instructional Resources, including Sound/Spelling Cards, Big Books (K-1), Vocabulary in Context Cards, Retelling Cards, and Language Support Cards, can be projected for interactive engagement and maximum impact.	**Leveled Readers,** with lesson plans developed by Irene Fountas, tie directly back to each week's core reading selection comprehension. They reinforce fluency, and provide practice in comparing, contrasting, and connecting reading selections on the same topic.
The ***Journeys* Assessment System** provides data to make informed instructional decisions and help students succeed. • Online administered and scored assessments evaluate and report progress. • Progress monitoring tools prescribe remediation, provide online feedback, and inform small-group instruction. • Weekly and Unit Assessments, along with Performance Tasks, prepare students for the next generation of online assessments. • The *Standards-Based Assessment Resource* includes technology-enhanced items and performance tasks. • The *Continuum Assessment System Benchmark Assessments* provide valid and reliable measures of student growth within and across grades.	**Options for Reteaching** in the Teacher's Edition offer another resource for differentiating instruction. Reteaching lessons in phonics, language arts, vocabulary, and comprehension strengthen skill acquisition for students who are either struggling, or who missed the core lesson.

Station Rotations	Individuals
Students can work collaboratively to respond to reading selections and complete performance tasks. They can also work together on **Literacy Center** activities, which include for each lesson: • Word Study • Think and Write • Comprehension and Fluency	**Student eBooks** provide the ultimate online experience. • Annotation and highlighting tools at point of use support close reading. • The integrated *my*Notebook allows students to take notes, copy and paste text from the eBook, and save the material for later performance tasks. • Students build fluency and comprehension using *Journeys* online Leveled Readers.
Performance Assessment resources give students an opportunity to work individually or collaboratively on the types of performance tasks they'll encounter on high-stakes assessments.	***my*WriteSmart** provides students with 21st-century resources for making direct connections between analytic reading and writing, as well as developing research and media skills. • Teachers can comment on student work during each step in the writing process. • Rubrics for both students and teachers are built into the tool, along with tools for planning, drafting, revising, and proofreading writing. **Interactive Lessons** in Writing and in Speaking and Listening provide students at Grades 3-6 an opportunity to review and enrich their growing knowledge independently through an engaging digital vehicle.
Online Leveled Readers and Vocabulary Readers build lesson-based comprehension, fluency, and word knowledge. • At stations, partners can read to one another and chart their fluency goals. • Online Vocabulary Readers used at stations allow students collaborative practice in applying vocabulary knowledge.	**The FYI site** provides real-world connections and fresh perspectives on unit topics with curated, contemporary informational text and media, motivating visuals, and recommended trade books for additional reading. Students can use these resources to make important connections for assigned or independent research.
Common Core Reading Practice and Assessment App provides engaging practice and develops skills needed for today's high-stakes assessments. • Fresh-read passages at correct Lexiles with increasing complexity throughout the year • Practice in standards-based test-taking skills • Tech-enhanced test items, such as drag-and-drop • Writing-based Performance Tasks • For teachers, real-time data on student progress • Other valuable student data, including number of attempts and number of right/wrong answers	**Ramp up student proficiency with authentic complex texts** • High-quality literary and informational texts, including numerous exemplars, in the Student Books • Full-length trade books, written by renowned authors

PACING GUIDE

Pacing Guide
Your *Journeys* Year at a Glance

BT: Benchmark Test
SA: Screening Assessment
UT: Unit Test

WT: Weekly Test
LT: Lesson Tool for Formative Assessment (*Language Workshop*)

Unit 1					Unit 2						Unit 3				
Lesson 1	Lesson 2	Lesson 3	Lesson 4	Lesson 5	Lesson 6	Lesson 7	Lesson 8	Lesson 9	Lesson 10	Extended Reading	Lesson 11	Lesson 12	Lesson 13	Lesson 14	Lesson 15
SA, WT	WT	WT	WT	WT, BT	WT	WT	WT	WT	WT, UT		WT	WT	WT	WT	WT, BT
LT	LT	LT	LT	LT	LT	LT	LT	LT	LT	LT	LT	LT	LT	LT	LT
Lesson 1	Lesson 2	Lesson 3	Lesson 4	Lesson 5	Lesson 6	Lesson 7	Lesson 8	Lesson 9	Lesson 10	Extended Reading	Lesson 11	Lesson 12	Lesson 13	Lesson 14	Lesson 15

(Left margin label: Language Workshop)

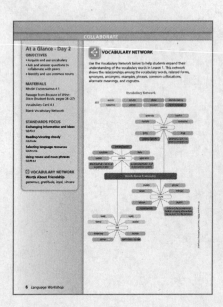

Language Workshop

An additional hour of daily instruction to support students' language acquisition.

Use the *Language Workshop Assessment Handbook* tools to monitor and assess students and provide them with the instruction they need, including measures of progress across proficiency levels.

CΟNTINUUM ASSESSMENTS

The **Continuum Assessment System Benchmark Assessments** provide valid and reliable measures of student growth within and across grades.

- Item difficulty adapts to each student
- Technology-enhanced item formats reflect and measure 21st-century skills and concepts
- Can be administered up to three times a year
- Aligned to the Common Core State Standards

- Weekly Tests (WT)

Benchmark and Unit Tests

- Benchmark Tests (BT)
- Unit Tests (UT)

Intervention Assessments

- Screening Assessments (SA)
- Diagnostic Assessments
- Progress-Monitoring Assessments

Unit 4						Unit 5					Unit 6					
Lesson 16	Lesson 17	Lesson 18	Lesson 19	Lesson 20	Extended Reading	Lesson 21	Lesson 22	Lesson 23	Lesson 24	Lesson 25	Lesson 26	Lesson 27	Lesson 28	Lesson 29	Lesson 30	Extended Reading
WT	WT	WT	WT	WT, UT		WT	WT	WT	WT	WT, BT	WT	WT	WT	WT	WT, UT	
LT	LT	LT	LT	LT	LT	LT	LT	LT	LT	LT	LT	LT	LT	LT	LT	LT
Lesson 16	Lesson 17	Lesson 18	Lesson 19	Lesson 20	Extended Reading	Lesson 21	Lesson 22	Lesson 23	Lesson 24	Lesson 25	Lesson 26	Lesson 27	Lesson 28	Lesson 29	Lesson 30	Extended Reading

HMH Decoding Power: Intensive Reading Instruction

Targeted support for students who need intensive intervention in one or more of the key foundational reading skills.

Intervention Assessments includes efficient, reliable tools to check that students are progressing toward grade-level achievement at an appropriate pace.

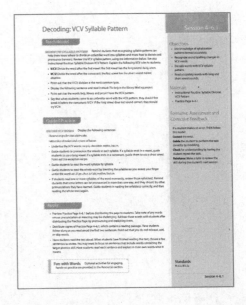

APPENDIX

Program Components Matrix

All print components are also available in digital formats.

Student-Facing Components

	Grade K	Grade 1	Grade 2	Grade 3	Grade 4	Grade 5	Grade 6
Alphafriends Cards	●						
Benchmark and Unit Tests Student Edition	●	●	●	●	●	●	●
Big Books	●	●					
Channel One News	●	●	●	●	●	●	●
Decodable Readers*		●	●				
FYI Site	●	●		●	●	●	●
GrammarSnap Videos		●		●	●	●	●
High-Frequency Word Cards	●	●	●				
HMH in the News	●	●	●	●	●	●	●
Interactive Lessons				●	●	●	●
Interactive Whiteboard Lessons	●	●	●	●	●	●	●
Language Support Cards	●	●	●		●	●	●
Letter, Word, Picture Cards	●						
Leveled Readers: Below-, On-, Above-Level, ELL	●	●		●	●	●	●
Literacy Centers	●	●		●	●	●	●
Multimedia Grammar Glossary		●		●	●	●	●
myNotebook		●	●	●	●	●	●
myWordList		●	●	●	●	●	●
myWriteSmart	●	●		●	●	●	●
Online Picture Card Bank	●	●		●	●	●	●
Performance Assessment				●	●	●	●
Punctuation Cards	●	●		●			
Read Aloud Books	●						
Reader's Notebook	●	●		●	●	●	●
Reading Adventure Student Magazine				●	●	●	●
Retelling Cards	●	●	●	●			
Sound/Spelling Cards	●	●	●	●			
Stream to Start Videos	●			●	●	●	●
Student Book	●	●			●	●	●
Student eBook	●	●		●	●	●	●
Student Online Resources	●	●	●	●	●	●	●
Trade Books		●	●	●	●	●	●
Vocabulary in Context Cards	●	●	●	●	●	●	●
Vocabulary Readers	●	●	●	●	●	●	●
Weekly Tests		●	●	●	●	●	●
Write-In Reader		●		●	●	●	●
Writing Handbook	●	●	●	●		●	●

Teaching-Facing Components

	Grade K	Grade 1	Grade 2	Grade 3	Grade 4	Grade 5	Grade 6
Benchmark and Unit Tests Teacher Edition	●	●	●	●	●	●	●
Blend-It Books		●					
Cold Reads		●	●	●	●	●	●
ELA Exemplar Teacher Resource	●	●	●	●	●	●	●
ELL Newcomer Teacher's Guide	●	●	●	●	●	●	●
ELL Teacher's Handbook	●	●	●	●	●	●	●
Grab-and-Go™ Resources	●	●	●	●	●	●	●
HMH Decoding Power: Intensive Reading Instruction	●	●	●	●	●	●	●
Instructional Card Kit	●	●	●	●	●	●	●
Interactive Instructional Flip Chart	●						
Intervention Assessments	●	●	●	●	●	●	●
Intervention Teaching Resources	●						
Language Workshop	●	●	●	●	●	●	●
Language Workshop Assessment Handbook	●	●	●	●	●		
Leveled Readers Teacher's Guides: Below-, On-, Above-Level, ELL	●	●	●	●	●	●	●
Literacy and Language Guide	●	●	●	●	●	●	●
My Journey Home: Family Connection	●	●	●	●	●	●	●
mySmartPlanner	●	●	●	●	●	●	●
Parent Resource	●	●	●	●	●	●	●
Performance Assessment Teacher's Guide				●	●	●	●
Professional Development Resources	●	●	●	●	●	●	●
Projectables	●	●	●	●	●	●	●
Quick Start Pacing Guide	●	●	●	●	●	●	●
Reader's Notebook Teacher's Guide	●	●	●	●	●	●	●
Standards-Based Assessment Resource	●	●	●	●	●	●	●
Teacher eBook	●	●	●	●	●	●	●
Teacher's Edition	●	●	●	●	●	●	●
Teacher Online Resources	●	●	●	●	●	●	●
Vocabulary Readers Teacher's Guides	●	●	●	●	●	●	●
Writing Handbook Teacher's Guide	●	●	●	●	●	●	●

Scope and Sequence for English Language Arts

READING LITERATURE AND INFORMATIONAL TEXT

	Kindergarten	Grade 1	Grade 2	Grade 3	Grade 4	Grade 5	Grade 6
Identify details	x						
Identify main idea and details	x	x	x	x	x	x	x
Analyze/evaluate text	x	x	x	x	x	x	x
*Make inferences and predictions	x	x	x	x	x	x	x
Monitor and clarify understanding	x	x	x	x	x	x	x
Ask and answer questions	x	x	x	x	x	x	x
Retell/summarize	x	x	x	x	x	x	x
Visualize	x	x	x	x	x	x	x
Understand cause and effect	x	x	x	x	x	x	x
Understand compare and contrast	x	x	x	x	x	x	x
Draw conclusions	x	x	x	x	x	x	x
Understand sequence of events	x	x	x	x	x	x	x
Understand story structure	x	x	x	x	x	x	x
Use text and illustrations/graphic features	x	x	x	x	x	x	x
Understand characters	x	x	x	x	x	x	x
Identify/describe narrative elements	x	x	x	x	x	x	x
Recognize common text types	x	x	x	x	x	x	x
Identify author/illustrator	x	x	x	x	x	x	x
Activate prior knowledge	x						
Identify sensory words		x	x	x	x	x	x
Read prose and poetry		x	x	x	x	x	x
Distinguish fact from opinion			x	x	x	x	x
Read and comprehend literature			x	x	x	x	x
Understand author's purpose			x	x	x	x	x
Understand theme				x	x	x	x
Make generalizations					x	x	x

FOUNDATIONAL SKILLS

	Kindergarten	Grade 1	Grade 2	Grade 3	Grade 4	Grade 5	Grade 6
Print Concepts							
Directionality	x						
Book parts and book handling	x						
Identify letters, words, and sentences	x						
Identify capitalization and punctuation	x						
Space between words	x						
Match oral words to printed words	x	x	x				
Graphics	x	x	x				
Types of print materials	x	x	x				

FOUNDATIONAL SKILLS (continued)

	Kindergarten	Grade 1	Grade 2	Grade 3	Grade 4	Grade 5	Grade 6
Phonological/Phonemic Awareness							
Understand that spoken words and syllables are made up of sequence of sounds	x						
Know the sounds of letters	x	x	x				
Initial, medial, and final sounds	x	x	x				
Blend phonemes to make words or syllables	x	x	x				
Segment phonemes in words	x	x	x				
Substitute or add phonemes in words	x	x	x				
Delete sound phonemes in words	x	x	x				
Distinguish between long- and short-vowel sounds	x	x	x				
Identify/produce rhyming words	x	x	x				
Track syllables	x	x	x				
Syllables in spoken words	x	x	x				
Match phonemes	x	x	x				
Phonics and Word Recognition							
Alphabetic principle	x	x					
Match consonant and short-vowel sounds to appropriate letters	x	x	x	x	x	x	x
Associate long-vowel sounds with common spellings	x	x	x	x	x	x	x
Understand that as letters in words change, so do the sounds	x	x	x	x	x	x	x
Blend sounds from letters and letter patterns into recognizable words	x	x	x	x	x	x	x
Vowel teams, diphthongs, and final -e	x	x	x	x	x	x	x
Initial/medial/final consonants	x	x	x	x	x	x	x
Consonant clusters/digraphs and silent consonants	x	x	x	x	x	x	x
R-controlled vowels	x	x	x	x	x	x	x
Schwa	x	x	x	x	x	x	x
Recognize common high-frequency words	x	x	x				
Decoding: Structural Analysis							
Phonograms/word families/onset-rimes	x	x					
Syllables and syllabication		x	x	x	x	x	x
Compound words		x	x	x	x	x	x
Contractions		x	x	x	x	x	x
Base words and inflected endings		x	x	x	x	x	x
Affixes		x	x	x	x	x	x
Greek and Latin roots						x	x
Stressed and unstressed syllables					x	x	x

Scope and Sequence for English Language Arts

FOUNDATIONAL SKILLS (continued)	Kindergarten	Grade 1	Grade 2	Grade 3	Grade 4	Grade 5	Grade 6
Fluency							
Read emergent texts with purpose/understanding	x						
Read on-level texts with purpose/understanding	x	x	x	x	x	x	x
Read aloud with accuracy	x	x	x	x	x	x	x
Read aloud with appropriate rate; adjust to purpose	x	x	x	x	x	x	x
Read aloud with expression	x	x	x	x	x	x	x
Read aloud with appropriate phrasing	x	x	x	x	x	x	x
Read aloud with appropriate intonation	x	x	x	x	x	x	x
Read aloud with appropriate stress		x	x	x	x	x	x
Use context to self-correct word recognition	x	x	x	x	x	x	x

WRITING	Kindergarten	Grade 1	Grade 2	Grade 3	Grade 4	Grade 5	Grade 6
Opinion Writing (Argument in Grade 6)							
State an opinion/point of view	x	x	x	x	x	x	x
Provide reasons/information for an opinion/ point of view		x	x	x	x	x	x
Use linking words to connect opinion and reasons		x	x	x	x	x	x
Provide a concluding statement			x	x	x	x	x
Opinion Writing Forms (Argument in Grade 6)							
Friendly letter, note, message	x						
Journal	x	x	x	x	x	x	
Response to literature	x	x	x	x	x	x	x
Opinion sentences/paragraph/ essay	x	x	x	x	x	x	x
Persuasive letter/essay			x	x	x	x	x
Problem and solution paragraph/composition					x	x	x	x
Public service announcement					x		
Editorial, persuasive argument						x	x
Book Review							x
Informative Writing							
Supply information/facts/details about a topic	x	x	x	x	x	x	x
Provide a sense of closure/concluding statement		x	x	x	x	x	x
Group related information together				x	x	x	x
Use linking words/phrases to connect ideas				x	x	x	x
Include formatting, visuals, multimedia to aid comprehension					x	x	x
Use precise language, domain-specific vocabulary					x	x	x

	Kindergarten	Grade 1	Grade 2	Grade 3	Grade 4	Grade 5	Grade 6
Informative Writing Forms							
Captions, invitations, lists	x						
Descriptive sentences	x	x					
Poetry		x					
Thank-you note		x					
Instructions/procedural composition		x	x	x	x		x
Informational sentences/paragraph(s)/essay		x	x	x	x	x	x
Report/research report	x	x	x	x	x	x	x
Summary, news report, journal entry					x	x	
Narrative Writing							
Tell about events in order and provide a reaction to what happened	x	x	x	x	x	x	x
Use temporal words to signal event order		x	x	x	x	x	x
Provide a sense of closure		x	x	x	x	x	x
Use details/dialogue to describe characters' actions, thoughts, feelings			x	x	x	x	x
Establish situation, narrator or characters, and natural event sequence				x	x	x	x
Narrative Writing Forms							
Names, labels, captions	x	x					
Sentences	x	x	x				
Story/fictional narrative	x	x	x	x	x	x	x
Personal narrative		x	x	x	x	x	x
Friendly letter		x	x	x	x	x	
Descriptive paragraph			x	x	x		
Dialogue				x	x	x	
Character description						x	
Autobiography						x	
Field Notes							x
Narrative Poem							x
Radio Script							x
Writing Traits							
Conventions	x	x	x	x	x	x	x
Purpose	x	x	x	x	x	x	x
Organization	x	x	x	x	x	x	x
Development	x	x	x	x	x	x	x
Elaboration	x	x	x	x	x	x	x

Scope and Sequence for English Language Arts

WRITING (continued)

	Kindergarten	Grade 1	Grade 2	Grade 3	Grade 4	Grade 5	Grade 6
Production and Distribution of Writing							
Writing process (prewrite, draft, revise, edit, publish)	x	x	x	x	x	x	x
Use digital tools to publish	x	x	x	x	x	x	x
Collaborate with peers	x	x	x	x	x	x	x
Match development and organization to task and purpose in writing			x	x	x	x	x
Use keyboarding skills					x	x	x	x
Research							
Participate in shared projects	x	x	x	x	x	x	x
Recall, gather information to answer a question			x	x	x	x	x
Write routinely over extended and shorter time frames			x	x	x	x	x
Conduct short research projects				x	x	x	x
Draw evidence from texts for analysis, reflection, research					x	x	x

SPEAKING AND LISTENING

	Kindergarten	Grade 1	Grade 2	Grade 3	Grade 4	Grade 5	Grade 6
Listening							
Respond to texts read aloud or media; paraphrase	x	x	x	x	x	x	x
Ask and answer questions of a speaker	x	x	x	x	x	x	x
Participate in collaborative groups	x	x	x	x	x	x	x
Follow discussion rules	x	x	x	x	x	x	x
Respond to a speaker by retelling and/or contributing information	x	x	x	x	x	x	x
Identify ideas and supporting evidence in oral presentations or texts read aloud	x	x	x	x	x	x	x
Draw and support conclusions about oral presentations or texts read aloud	x	x	x	x	x	x	x
Identify and interpret purpose, central idea, and key points in oral presentations or texts read aloud	x	x	x	x	x	x	x
Follow multiple-step oral directions	x	x	x	x	x	x	x
Analyze media sources	x	x	x	x	x	x	x
Analyze persuasive techniques				x	x	x	x
Speaking							
Participate in collaborative groups to discuss topics and texts	x	x	x	x	x	x	x
Follow discussion rules	x	x	x	x	x	x	x
Build on others' comments in conversations	x	x	x	x	x	x	x
Ask and answer questions of a speaker	x	x	x	x	x	x	x
Present descriptions of people, places, things, and events	x	x					
Memorize and recite poems, rhymes, songs, and speeches		x				x	x

SPEAKING AND LISTENING (continued)

	Kindergarten	Grade 1	Grade 2	Grade 3	Grade 4	Grade 5	Grade 6
Retell a story/experience in a narrative presentation, including dramatization		X	X	X			
Use visual displays or media (including audio) in presentations	X	X	X	X	X	X	X
Create recordings of stories/poems			X				
Give informative presentations	X	X	X	X	X	X	X
Give opinion presentations					X	X	X
Differentiate between formal and informal English; adapt to task and situation		X	X	X	X	X	X
Select a focus and organizational structure for a presentation			X	X	X	X	X

LANGUAGE

	Kindergarten	Grade 1	Grade 2	Grade 3	Grade 4	Grade 5	Grade 6
Sentences							
Interrogatives	X	X	X	X	X	X	X
Complete sentences	X	X	X	X	X	X	X
Kinds of sentences		X	X	X	X	X	X
Compound sentences		X	X	X	X	X	X
Complex sentences				X	X	X	X
Transitions						X	X
Grammar							
Nouns (common, proper, singular, regular plural)	X	X	X	X	X	X	X
Nouns (possessive, abbreviations, appositives)		X	X	X	X	X	X
Nouns (collective, irregular plurals)			X	X	X	X	X
Nouns (abstract)				X	X	X	X
Verbs (action, helping, linking, transitive, intransitive, regular, irregular)	X	X	X	X	X	X	X
Subject-Verb Agreement	X	X	X	X	X	X	X
Verb Tenses (present, past, future)	X	X	X	X	X	X	X
Verb Tenses (progressive)					X	X	X
Verb Tenses (present, past, and future perfect)						X	X
Modal Auxiliaries					X	X	X
Participles; infinitives					X	X	X
Negatives					X	X	X
Adjectives (common, proper, articles, demonstrative, comparative, superlative)		X	X	X	X	X	X
Adjective order					X	X	X
Adverbs (place, time, manner, degree)		X	X	X	X	X	X
Adverbs (relative)					X	X	X
Pronouns (subject, object, possessive, indefinite)	X	X	X	X	X	X	X

Scope and Sequence for English Language Arts

LANGUAGE (continued)	Kindergarten	Grade 1	Grade 2	Grade 3	Grade 4	Grade 5	Grade 6
Grammar (continued)							
Pronouns (reflexive, demonstrative, antecedents)			x	x	x	x	x
Pronouns (reciprocal, interrogative, relative; agreement)				x	x	x	x
Prepositions, prepositional phrases	x	x	x	x	x	x	x
Conjunctions		x	x	x	x	x	x
Conjunctions (coordinating and subordinating)				x	x	x	x
Conjunctions (correlative)						x	x
Contractions, abbreviations		x	x	x	x	x	x
Punctuation							
End punctuation	x	x	x	x	x	x	x
Commas in dates, places, in a series			x	x	x	x	x
Commas in greetings, closings of letters			x	x	x	x	x
Commas in addresses, dialogue, compound sentences				x	x	x	x
Commas in introductory elements						x	x
Direct quotations, dialogue			x	x	x	x	x
Interjections						x	x
Apostrophes in contractions and possessives		x	x	x	x	x	x
Quotations and underlining in titles					x	x	x
Semicolons						x	x
Capitalization							
First word in a sentence, names of people, pronoun *I*	x	x	x	x	x	x	x
Dates		x	x	x	x	x	x
Holidays, product names, geographic names		x	x	x	x	x	x
Titles		x	x	x	x	x	x
Spelling							
Spell simple words phonetically	x	x					
Write most consonants and short-vowel sounds	x	x					
Spell irregular words		x	x	x	x	x	x
Spell words using generalized spelling patterns			x	x	x	x	x
Check spelling using reference materials			x	x	x	x	x
Add suffixes to base words				x	x	x	x
Handwriting							
Print/write legibly	x	x	x	x	x	x	x

LANGUAGE (continued)

	Kindergarten	Grade 1	Grade 2	Grade 3	Grade 4	Grade 5	Grade 6
Language Knowledge							
Compare formal and informal English uses			x	x	x	x	x
Choose words and phrases for effect				x	x	x	x
Recognize conventions of spoken and written English				x	x	x	x
Rework sentences for meaning, audience, purpose			x	x	x	x	x
Compare/contrast varieties of Englishh						x	x
Vocabulary Acquisition and Use							
Use context to determine/clarify word meaning	x	x	x	x	x	x	x
Use inflections to determine/clarify word meaning	x	x	x	x	x	x	x
Use affixes/root words to determine/clarify word meaning	x	x	x	x	x	x	x
Sort words into categories	x	x					
Shades of meaning	x	x	x	x	x	x	x
Expand vocabulary through speaking, reading, listening, responding	x	x	x	x	x	x	x
Real-life connection between words and their use	x	x	x	x	x	x	x
Use word relationships to clarify word meaning (synonyms, antonyms, spatial and temporal relationships)	x	x	x	x	x	x	x
Use precise words	x	x	x	x	x	x	x
Use topic-based words	x	x	x	x	x	x	x
Use glossaries/dictionaries to determine/clarify word meaning			x	x	x	x	x
Distinguish between literal and non-literal meanings of words				x	x	x	x
Use thesauruses to determine/clarify word meaning					x	x	x
Use Greek/Latin word parts to determine/clarify word meaning					x	x	x
Explain similes and metaphors					x	x	x
Explain idioms, adages, proverbs					x	x	x

Scope and Sequence for English Language Development
Language Workshop

Interact in Meaningful Ways

COLLABORATIVE	
Skill	**Subskill**
basic social communication	agree and disagree
	ask for assistance or permission
	express feelings or needs
	greet
	express likes and dislikes
	apologize
	give instructions
exchanging information and ideas	respond using gestures, words, and phrases
	ask and answer *yes-no* questions
	ask and answer *wh-* questions
	listen attentively
	follow turn-taking rules
	ask relevant questions
	affirm others
	add relevant information
	build on responses
	provide useful feedback
interacting via written English	collaboration in joint composing projects
	use technology where appropriate
offering opinions	offer opinions and ideas using learned phrases
	offer opinions and ideas using open responses
	gain and/or hold the floor
	add information to/elaborate on an idea
	negotiate with others in a conversation
	provide counterarguments
	persuade others in conversation
adapting language choices	recognize that language choices vary according to social setting
	adjust language choices according to purpose, task, and audience

LANGUAGE PROFICIENCY LEVELS

Em (Emerging) **Ex** (Expanding) **Br** (Bridging)

	Grade K			Grade 1			Grade 2			Grade 3			Grade 4			Grade 5			Grade 6		
	Em	Ex	Br	Em	Ex	Br	Em	Ex	Br	Em	Ex	Br	Em	Ex	Br	Em	Ex	Br	Em	Ex	Br
	x	x	x	x	x	x	x			x			x			x			x		
	x	x	x	x	x		x			x			x			x			x		
	x	x	x	x	x	x	x			x			x			x			x		
	x	x	x	x	x		x			x			x			x			x		
	x	x	x	x	x		x			x			x			x			x		
	x	x	x	x	x	x	x			x			x			x			x		
	x	x	x	x	x		x			x			x			x			x		
	x			x			x			x			x			x			x		
	x	x	x	x	x		x			x			x			x			x		
	x	x	x	x	x	x	x			x			x			x			x		
		x	x		x	x		x	x												
		x	x		x	x		x	x		x	x		x	x		x	x		x	x
								x	x		x	x		x	x		x	x		x	x
								x	x		x	x		x	x		x	x		x	x
								x	x		x	x		x	x		x	x		x	x
									x			x			x			x			x
									x			x			x			x			x
	x	x	x	x	x	x	x	x	x	x	x	x	x	x	x	x	x	x	x	x	x
	x	x	x	x	x	x	x	x	x	x	x	x	x	x	x	x	x	x	x	x	x
	x	x	x	x	x	x	x	x	x	x	x	x	x	x	x						
	x	x	x	x	x	x	x	x	x												
		x	x	x	x	x	x	x	x	x	x	x	x	x	x	x	x	x	x	x	x
			x		x	x			x			x			x			x			x
					x	x	x	x	x	x	x	x	x	x	x	x	x	x	x	x	x
						x		x	x		x	x		x	x		x	x		x	x
													x	x	x	x	x	x	x	x	x
					x		x			x	x		x	x							
								x	x		x	x	x	x	x	x	x	x	x	x	x

Scope and Sequence for English Language Development
Language Workshop

Interact in Meaningful Ways

INTERPRETIVE	
Skill	**Subskill**
listening actively	ask and answer *yes-no*, and *wh-* questions with oral sentence frames
	ask and answer questions with oral sentence frames
	ask and answer detailed questions to demonstrate active listening
	ask and answer basic questions to demonstrate active listening
reading/viewing closely	describe ideas, phenomena, and text elements
	determine meaning of unknown words using knowledge of morphology, linguistic context, reference materials, and visual cues
evaluating language choices	describe the language an author uses to present or support an idea
	describe how well an author or speaker uses specific language to present an idea or support an opinion
analyzing language choices	distinguish how different words are used to produce different effects
	distinguish how different words with similar meanings produce shades of meaning and a different effect
	distingusih how figurative language produces shades of meaning and different effects

LANGUAGE PROFICIENCY LEVELS

Em (Emerging) **Ex** (Expanding) **Br** (Bridging)

	Grade K			Grade 1			Grade 2			Grade 3			Grade 4			Grade 5			Grade 6		
	Em	Ex	Br	Em	Ex	Br	Em	Ex	Br	Em	Ex	Br	Em	Ex	Br	Em	Ex	Br	Em	Ex	Br
	x			x	x																
		x				x	x	x													
			x			x		x	x		x	x		x	x		x	x		x	x
				x	x		x			x			x			x			x		
	x	x	x	x	x	x	x	x	x	x	x	x	x	x	x	x	x	x	x	x	x
													x	x	x	x	x	x	x	x	x
	x	x	x	x	x	x	x	x													
									x	x	x	x	x	x	x	x	x	x	x	x	x
	x			x			x			x	x	x	x				x	x	x	x	x
		x	x		x	x		x	x	x	x			x	x		x	x		x	x
														x	x		x	x		x	x

Scope and Sequence for English Language Development
Language Workshop

Interact in Meaningful Ways

PRODUCTIVE

Skill	Subskill
presenting	plan and deliver oral presentations
composing/writing	write literary texts collaboratively
	write informational texts collaboratively
	write literary texts independently
	write informational texts independently
	recount experiences
	paraphrase/retell texts
	write summaries using complete sentences and key words
	use appropriate text organization
	use growing understanding of register
supporting opinions	support opinions by providing good reasons or some textual evidence or background knowledge
	persuade others by providing good reasons and detailed textual evidence
	use modal expressions to express ideas, attitude, and opinions or to temper statements
	use phrasing to express ideas, attitude, and opinions or to temper statements
selecting language resources	retell texts using a select set of key words
	recount experiences using a select set of key words
	retell texts using complete sentences and key words
	recount experiences using complete sentences and key words
	retell texts using increasingly detailed complete sentences
	recount experiences using increasingly detailed complete sentences
	use general academic and domain-specific words to add details
	use general academic and domain-specific words to create shades of meaning
	use general academic and domain-specific words to create effect and precision
	use synonyms to create effect, shades of meaning, or precision
	use antonyms to create effect, shades of meaning, or precision
	use non-literal language to create effect, shades of meaning, or precision
	select and use affixes for accuracy and precision

	Grade K			Grade 1			Grade 2			Grade 3			Grade 4			Grade 5			Grade 6		
	Em	Ex	Br	Em	Ex	Br	Em	Ex	Br	Em	Ex	Br	Em	Ex	Br	Em	Ex	Br	Em	Ex	Br
	x	x	x	x	x	x	x	x	x	x	x	x	x	x	x	x	x	x	x	x	x
	x	x	x	x	x	x	x	x	x	x	x	x	x	x	x	x	x	x	x	x	x
	x	x	x	x	x	x	x	x	x	x	x	x	x	x	x	x	x	x	x	x	x
		x	x		x	x	x	x	x	x	x	x	x	x	x	x	x	x	x	x	x
		x	x		x	x	x	x	x	x	x	x	x	x	x	x	x	x	x	x	x
										x	x	x	x	x	x	x	x	x	x	x	x
										x	x	x	x	x	x	x	x	x	x	x	x
													x	x	x	x	x	x	x	x	x
											x	x		x	x		x	x		x	x
												x		x			x			x
	x	x	x	x	x	x	x	x	x	x	x	x	x	x	x	x	x	x	x	x	x
									x			x		x	x		x	x		x	x
													x	x	x	x	x	x	x	x	x
															x			x			x
	x			x			x														
	x			x			x														
		x			x			x													
		x			x			x													
			x			x			x												
			x			x			x												
	x	x		x	x	x	x	x		x	x		x	x	x	x	x	x	x	x	x
		x	x		x	x		x			x	x		x	x		x	x		x	x
			x		x	x		x	x		x	x	x	x	x	x	x	x	x	x	x
			x			x			x			x		x	x		x	x		x	x
			x			x			x			x		x	x		x	x		x	x
			x			x			x			x			x			x			x
													x	x	x	x	x	x	x	x	x

Scope and Sequence for English Language Development
Language Workshop

Learning About How English Works

STRUCTURING COHESIVE TEXTS

Skill	Subskill
understanding text structure	apply understanding of text organization to comprehend and compose texts
understanding cohesion	apply understanding of links (ideas, events, reasons) within a text to comprehend and compose texts
	apply understanding of connecting words to comprehend and compose texts
	apply understanding of language resources that refer reader back or forward in a text to comprehend and compose texts
	apply understanding of personal pronouns
	apply understanding of possessive pronouns
	apply understanding of indefinite pronouns
	apply understanding of reflexive pronouns

EXPANDING AND ENRICHING IDEAS

using verbs and verb phrases	use verbs and verb types in shared language activities
	use verb tenses to convey time
	recognize and use present tense
	recognize and use past tense
	recognize and use future tense
	recognize and use irregular past tense
using nouns and noun phrases	expand noun phrases to enrich meaning and add details
	recognize and use common nouns
	recognize and use proper nouns
	recognize and use regular plural nouns
	recognize and use adjectives
	recognize and use irregular plural nouns
	recognize and use possessive nouns
	recognize and use collective nouns
	recognize and use comparative and superlative adjectives
modifying to add details	expand sentences with prepositions to provide detail
	expand sentences with prepositional phrases to provide detail
	expand sentences with adverbs to provide detail
	expand sentences with adverb phrases to provide detail
	recognize and use comparative and superlative adverbs

LANGUAGE PROFICIENCY LEVELS

Em (Emerging) **Ex** (Expanding) **Br** (Bridging)

	Grade K			Grade 1			Grade 2			Grade 3			Grade 4			Grade 5			Grade 6		
	Em	Ex	Br	Em	Ex	Br	Em	Ex	Br	Em	Ex	Br	Em	Ex	Br	Em	Ex	Br	Em	Ex	Br
	x	x	x	x	x	x	x	x	x	x	x	x	x	x	x	x	x	x	x	x	x
	x	x	x	x	x	x	x	x	x	x	x	x	x	x	x	x	x	x	x	x	x
	x	x	x	x	x	x	x	x	x	x	x	x	x	x	x	x	x	x	x	x	x
							x	x	x	x	x	x	x	x	x	x	x	x	x	x	x
							x	x	x	x	x	x	x	x	x	x	x	x	x	x	x
							x	x	x	x	x	x	x	x	x	x	x	x	x	x	x
							x	x	x	x	x	x	x	x	x	x	x	x	x	x	x
							x	x	x	x	x	x	x	x	x	x	x	x	x	x	x

	Grade K			Grade 1			Grade 2			Grade 3			Grade 4			Grade 5			Grade 6		
	Em	Ex	Br	Em	Ex	Br	Em	Ex	Br	Em	Ex	Br	Em	Ex	Br	Em	Ex	Br	Em	Ex	Br
	x	x	x	x	x	x	x	x	x	x	x	x	x	x	x	x	x	x	x	x	x
	x	x	x	x	x	x	x	x	x	x	x	x	x	x	x	x	x	x	x	x	x
	x	x	x	x	x	x	x	x	x	x	x	x	x	x	x	x	x	x	x	x	x
	x	x	x	x	x	x	x	x	x	x	x	x	x	x	x	x	x	x	x	x	x
			x			x			x		x	x		x	x	x	x	x	x	x	x
									x		x	x		x	x	x	x	x	x	x	x
	x	x	x	x	x	x	x	x	x	x	x	x	x	x	x	x	x	x	x	x	x
	x	x	x	x	x	x	x	x	x	x	x	x	x	x	x	x	x	x	x	x	x
	x	x	x	x	x	x	x	x	x	x	x	x	x	x	x	x	x	x	x	x	x
	x	x	x	x	x	x	x	x	x	x	x	x	x	x	x	x	x	x	x	x	x
	x	x	x	x	x	x	x	x	x	x	x	x	x	x	x	x	x	x	x	x	x
			x			x			x		x	x	x	x	x	x	x	x	x	x	x
						x			x		x	x	x	x	x	x	x	x	x	x	x
									x		x	x	x	x	x	x	x	x	x	x	x
									x		x	x	x	x	x	x	x	x	x	x	x
	x	x	x	x	x	x	x	x	x	x	x	x	x	x	x	x	x	x	x	x	x
	x	x	x	x	x	x	x	x	x	x	x	x	x	x	x	x	x	x	x	x	x
									x	x	x	x	x	x	x	x	x	x	x	x	x
									x	x	x	x	x	x	x	x	x	x	x	x	x
										x	x	x	x	x	x	x	x	x	x	x	x

Scope and Sequence for English Language Development
Language Workshop

Learning About How English Works

CONNECTING AND CONDENSING IDEAS	
Skill	**Subskill**
connecting ideas	create compound sentences using coordinate conjunctions to make connections and join ideas
	combine clauses to express cause and effect
	create compound and complex sentences
	combine clauses to make a concession
	combine clauses to link two ideas that happen at the same time
	understand and use subordinate conjunctions
	combine clauses to provide evidence to support ideas or opinions
condensing ideas	condense clauses in simple ways to create precise and detailed sentences
	condense clauses by embedding clauses to create precise and detailed sentences

Word-Learning Strategies

Skill	**Subskill**
using word-learning strategies	word relationships
	bases
	roots
	affixes: prefixes and suffixes
	inflectional endings
	context clues
	shades of meaning
	antonyms
	synonyms
	homophones
	compound words
	multiple-meaning words
	figurative language
	idioms

	Grade K			Grade 1			Grade 2			Grade 3			Grade 4			Grade 5			Grade 6		
	Em	Ex	Br	Em	Ex	Br	Em	Ex	Br	Em	Ex	Br	Em	Ex	Br	Em	Ex	Br	Em	Ex	Br
	x	x	x	x	x	x	x	x	x	x			x			x			x		
		x	x		x	x		x	x		x	x		x	x		x	x		x	x
			x			x			x		x	x		x	x		x	x		x	x
									x		x	x		x	x		x	x		x	x
												x			x	x	x	x	x	x	x
														x	x		x	x		x	x
																x	x	x	x	x	x
				x	x	x	x	x	x	x			x			x			x		
					x	x		x	x		x	x	x	x	x	x	x	x	x	x	x

	Em	Ex	Br	Em	Ex	Br	Em	Ex	Br	Em	Ex	Br	Em	Ex	Br	Em	Ex	Br	Em	Ex	Br
	x	x	x	x	x	x	x	x	x												
										x	x	x	x	x	x	x	x	x	x	x	x
				x	x	x	x	x	x	x	x	x	x	x	x	x	x	x	x	x	x
	x	x	x	x	x	x	x	x	x	x	x	x	x	x	x	x	x	x	x	x	x
	x	x	x	x	x	x	x	x	x	x	x	x	x	x	x	x	x	x	x	x	x
				x	x	x	x	x	x	x	x			x	x	x	x	x	x	x	x
											x	x	x	x	x	x	x	x	x	x	x
	x	x	x	x	x	x	x	x	x		x	x	x	x	x	x	x	x	x	x	x
	x	x	x	x	x	x	x	x	x		x	x	x	x	x	x	x	x	x	x	x
	x	x	x	x	x	x	x	x	x		x	x	x	x	x	x	x	x	x	x	x
	x	x	x	x	x	x	x	x	x	x	x	x	x	x	x	x	x	x	x	x	x
	x	x	x	x	x	x	x	x	x	x	x	x	x	x	x	x	x	x	x	x	x
										x	x	x		x	x		x	x		x	x
	x	x	x	x	x	x	x	x	x	x	x	x	x	x	x	x	x	x	x	x	x

Scope and Sequence for English Language Development
Language Workshop

Writing Products

Skill	Subskill
Informational Text Types	description
	procedure
	recount
	informational report
	explanation
	exposition
	response
Literary Text Types	story
	drama
	poetry
	retelling a story

	Grade K			Grade 1			Grade 2			Grade 3			Grade 4			Grade 5			Grade 6		
	Em	Ex	Br	Em	Ex	Br	Em	Ex	Br	Em	Ex	Br	Em	Ex	Br	Em	Ex	Br	Em	Ex	Br
	x	x	x	x	x	x	x	x	x	x	x	x	x	x	x	x	x	x	x	x	x
	x	x	x	x	x	x	x	x	x	x	x	x	x	x	x	x	x	x	x	x	x
	x	x	x	x	x	x	x	x	x	x	x	x	x	x	x	x	x	x	x	x	x
	x	x	x	x	x	x	x	x	x	x	x	x	x	x	x	x	x	x	x	x	x
	x	x	x	x	x	x	x	x	x	x	x	x	x	x	x	x	x	x	x	x	x
	x	x	x	x	x	x	x	x	x	x	x	x	x	x	x	x	x	x	x	x	x
	x	x	x	x	x	x	x	x	x	x	x	x	x	x	x	x	x	x	x	x	x
	x	x	x	x	x	x	x	x	x	x	x	x	x	x	x	x	x	x	x	x	x
	x	x	x	x	x	x	x	x	x	x	x	x	x	x	x	x	x	x	x	x	x
	x	x	x	x	x	x	x	x	x	x	x	x	x	x	x	x	x	x	x	x	x
	x	x	x	x	x	x	x	x	x	x	x	x	x	x	x	x	x	x	x	x	x

Linguistic Contrast and Transfer

Linguistic Contrastive Analysis

Linguistic contrastive analysis is the study of similarities and differences among languages. When students have diverse language backgrounds, it is helpful for the teacher to know which sounds and features of English may pose difficulty. The teacher can then take the time to provide additional practice with these sounds and features.

The Linguistic Contrastive Analysis Charts on the following pages outline some of the features of English that may pose special challenges for speakers of other first languages. The charts, of course, are not exhaustive; nor should they be taken to mean that linguistic diversity brings only challenges to the classroom. The languages of students' families and communities are assets to celebrate and draw upon; students who grow up learning in, and about, more than one language gain knowledge about the nature of language itself while preparing for the life-enriching opportunities provided by biliteracy.

Linguistic Transfer Challenges

The phonology, semantics, morphology, and syntax of the English language may be more or less challenging for students depending on their first languages and how those languages compare to English in these respects. For example, some speech sounds that are commonly used in English are not used at all in other languages. Some English sentence structures, too, may not exist in a student's first language—or the structure may be slightly different. In addition, the alphabetic writing system and directionality of print in English, though familiar to English learners whose first language also uses a Roman alphabet (such as Spanish, Vietnamese, or American Sign Language), may pose special challenges for students whose linguistic background is Arabic or Chinese.

Clearly, challenges and opportunities related to linguistic diversity abound, for both students and teachers. In addition to the charts on these pages, assistance for providing linguistically appropriate transfer support is provided in point-of-use notes throughout the instruction in *Journeys*.

Positive Transfer

It is also helpful for teachers to know that many kinds of skills and knowledge do transfer readily across languages. Thinking skills, comprehension skills, content knowledge, an understanding of social register (that is, when it is appropriate to address another formally versus informally): these are skills that a English learner may bring to the classroom, and these skills can and do transfer into English. Like all students, English learners may need focused instruction in academic English in order to demonstrate such skills and engage in academic discourse.

Positive transfer can also expedite the early stages of reading and writing in English. Students who are phonologically aware and have learned to decode in their first language have gained critical understandings about the sounds of speech and the connections of speech to print. This knowledge will accelerate their acquisition of written English.

Phonological Features

ENGLISH	SPANISH	VIETNAMESE	CANTONESE OR MANDARIN	PILIPINO OR TAGALOG	HMONG	KOREAN
Initial Consonants						
/f/ fan	Little difficulty	/b/ ban	Little difficulty	/p/ pan	/p/ pan	/p/ pan
/v/ van	/b/, /f/ ban, fan (Note: Spanish has only one sound for /b/ and /v/.)	Little difficulty	/w/ wan	Little difficulty	Little difficulty	/w/, /b/ wan, ban
/th/ though	Little difficulty	/d/ doe	/d/ doe (Note: /th/ and /th/ do not exist.)	/b/, /f/ bow, foe	/d/ doe	/z/ zo (Note: /th/ and /th/ do not exist.)
/th/ think	/d/ dink	/d/, /z/ dink, zink	/d/ dink	/d/ dink	/d/ dink	/s/ sink
/sh/ sheet	/ch/ cheat (Note: /sh/ does not exist.)	/s/, /ch/ seat, cheat	/s/ seat	Little difficulty	Little difficulty	Little difficulty
/j/ jar	/h/, /y/ har, yar	/z/ zar	Little difficulty	/y/ yar	Little difficulty	/zh/ as in rouge
/y/ yes	/j/ jes	Little difficulty	Little difficulty	Little difficulty	Little difficulty	Little difficulty
/h/ house	The nearest sound to /h/ in Spanish sounds like the *ch* in **Bach**.	Little difficulty	The nearest sound to /h/ sounds like the *ch* in **Bach**.	Little difficulty	Little difficulty	Little difficulty
/n/ need	Little difficulty	Little difficulty	/l/ lead	Little difficulty	Little difficulty	Little difficulty
/r/ rock	rolled or trilled Rock	Little difficulty	/l/ lock (Note: Many speakers find /l/ and /r/ difficult to distinguish.)	Little difficulty	Little difficulty	lock (Note: /r/ does not exist.)
/s/ student	add /e/ before /s/ estudent	Little difficulty	Little difficulty	Little difficulty	Little difficulty	/sh/ shtudent
/z/ zoo	/s/ sue (Note: Initial /z/ does not exist.)	Little difficulty	/s/ sue (Note: /z/ does not exist.)	/s/ sue	/s/ sue	/j/, /ch/ choo
/p/, /t/, /k/ pot, tot, cot	/b/, /d/, /g/ bot, dot, got	Initial /t/ in Vietnamese sounds like /d/: dot	Little difficulty	/b/, /d/, /g/ bot, dot, got	Little difficulty	/p/ may be replaced by /f/: fought
/b/, /d/, /g/ bet, debt, get	Initial /b/ is sometimes replaced with /v/: vet	Little difficulty	/p/, /t/, /k/ pet, tet, ket	Little difficulty	Little difficulty	/b/ may be replaced by /v/: vet

Phonological Features

ENGLISH	SPANISH	VIETNAMESE	CANTONESE OR MANDARIN	PILIPINO OR TAGALOG	HMONG	KOREAN
Medial Consonants						
/zh/ measure	/z/ mezure	Little difficulty	/z/, /sh/ mezure, meashure	/z/ mezure	Little difficulty	/z/, /sh/ mezure, meashure
/r/ horrible	rolled or trilled hoRrible	Little difficulty	/l/ holible	Little difficulty	Little difficulty	/l/ holible
Final Consonants						
/p/, /k/, /t/ tip, sick, sit	Little difficulty	Little difficulty	Often dropped or replaced with a schwa sound. (Note: there are few final consonants.)	Little difficulty	/b/, /d/, /g/ tib, sid, sig	Often dropped or replaced with a schwa sound. (Note: there are few final consonants.)
/s/ after consonant cats, hats	Little difficulty	Not used in Vietnamese	Little difficulty	Little difficulty	Little difficulty	May be deleted
/v/ love	Usually no difficulty, but may be replaced with /b/: lub	/b/, /p/ lub, lup	Often deleted	Little difficulty	Often deleted	Little difficulty, but may be replaced by /b/ lub
/j/ edge	/ch/ etch	Often deleted	Little difficulty	/ə/ added at end edgeh	Little difficulty	/ə/ added at end edgeh
/m/ dream	/n/, /ng/ drean, dreang	Little difficulty	Little difficulty	Little difficulty	Little difficulty	Little difficulty
/ng/ thing	/n/ thin	Little difficulty	Little difficulty	/n/ thin	Little difficulty	Little difficulty
Vowels						
/ē/ sheep	Little difficulty	Little difficulty	Little difficulty	Little difficulty	Little difficulty	Little difficulty
/i/ lip	/ē/ leap	/ē/ leap	Little difficulty	/ē/ leap	Little difficulty	/ē/ leap
/ā/ raid	Often substitute /e/: red	Little difficulty	Little difficulty	Little difficulty	Little difficulty	/e/ red
/e/ bet	/ā/ bait	/a/ bat	Vowel sounds might vary as a function of the surrounding consonant sounds.	/ā/ bait	Little difficulty	/ē/ beat
/a/ cat	/o/ cot	/o/ cot	/a/ does not exist: ket, cut, cot Most frequently substitute /a/ with /e/.	/o/ cot	/o/ cot	Little difficulty

Phonological Features

ENGLISH	SPANISH	VIETNAMESE	CANTONESE OR MANDARIN	PILIPINO OR TAGALOG	HMONG	KOREAN
Vowels (*continued*)						
/o/ cl**o**ck	/ō/ cl**oa**k	Little difficulty	Little difficulty	/ō/ cl**oa**k	Little difficulty	/ō/ cl**oa**k (There are no long/short vowel distinctions in Korean.)
/ə/ **a**bove	Does not exist. Often replaced by another vowel.	Little difficulty	Does not exist. Often replaced by another vowel.	Does not exist. Often replaced by another vowel.	Does not exist. Often replaced by another vowel.	Does not exist. Often replaced by another vowel.
/u/ c**u**p	/o/, /ōō/ c**o**p, c**oo**p	Little difficulty	/o/ c**o**p	/o/ c**o**p	Little difficulty	/o/ c**o**p
/ō/ b**oa**t	Little difficulty	Little difficulty	Little difficulty	Little difficulty	/ô/ b**ough**t	Little difficulty
/ōō/ p**u**ll	/ōō/ p**oo**l	/ōō/ p**oo**l	/ōō/ p**oo**l	/ōō/ p**oo**l	Little difficulty	Little difficulty
/7/ p**oo**l	Little difficulty	Little difficulty	Little difficulty	Little difficulty	Little difficulty	Little difficulty

Grammatical Features

GRAMMAR POINT	SPANISH	VIETNAMESE	CANTONESE OR MANDARIN	PILIPINO OR TAGALOG	HMONG	KOREAN
Nouns						
PLURAL FORMS Nouns do not change form to show the plural in the primary language or plurals are not used in the same way.		●	●		●	●
POSSESSIVE FORMS Possessives are either inferred or are not formed in the same way.	●	●	●	●	●	●
The word order in the primary language is different.	●	●	●	●	●	●
COUNT VS. NONCOUNT Nouns that are count and noncount differ between English and the primary language.	●	●	●	●	●	●
Articles						
Articles are either lacking or the distinction between *a* and *the* is not paralleled in the primary language.		●	●	●	●	●
Learners sometimes confuse the articles *a/an* with *one* since articles either do not exist in the primary language or serve a different function.		●			●	

Grammatical Features

GRAMMAR POINT	SPANISH	VIETNAMESE	CANTONESE OR MANDARIN	PILIPINO OR TAGALOG	HMONG	KOREAN
Pronouns						
PERSONAL PRONOUNS, GENDER The third person pronoun in the primary language is gender-free. The same pronoun is used where English uses masculine, feminine, and neuter pronouns, resulting in confusion of pronoun forms in English.			●	●	●	
PERSONAL PRONOUN FORMS The same pronoun form is used for he/him, she/her, and in some primary languages for I/me and we/us.			●		●	
There is no number agreement in the primary language. In Vietnamese, plurality is never expressed.		●	●			
Subject pronouns may be dropped in the primary language and the verb ending supplies information on number and/or gender.	●					
Direct objects are frequently dropped in the primary language.		●				
A subordinate clause at the beginning of a sentence does not require a subject in the primary language.		●	●			●
(Use of pronouns with subject nouns) This type of redundant structure reflects the "topic-comment" approach used in the primary language: The speaker mentions a topic and then makes a comment on it.	●	●	●		●	●
It is common in the primary language to repeat nouns rather than to use pronouns.		●	●			●
POSSESSIVE FORMS Speakers tend to omit final *n*, creating confusion between *my* and *mine*.		●	●		●	●
Verbs						
SUBJECT–VERB AGREEMENT There is no subject-verb agreement in the primary language.		●	●	●	●	●
TENSE Verb forms do not change to indicate tense, or time is understood from context.		●	●	●	●	●
PAST TENSE Speakers of the primary language have difficulty recognizing that merely a vowel shift in the middle of the verb, rather than a change in the ending of the verb, is sufficient to produce a change of tense in irregular verbs.	●	●	●		●	●

Grammatical Features

GRAMMAR POINT	SPANISH	VIETNAMESE	CANTONESE OR MANDARIN	PILIPINO OR TAGALOG	HMONG	KOREAN
Verbs *(continued)*						
IN NEGATIVE STATEMENTS Helping verbs are not used in negative statements in the primary language.	●		●	●		● (There are no helping verbs in Korean.)
VERB TENSE The verb form either doesn't exist in the primary language or has a different function. Vietnamese, Hmong, Cantonese, and Mandarin do not have verbs to express time.		●	●	●	●	●
PAST CONTINUOUS In the primary language, the past continuous form can be used in contexts in which English uses the expression *used to* or the simple past.	●			●		
VERB AS A NOUN Unlike English, Cantonese does not require an infinitive marker when using a verb as a noun.			●			
In Hmong, verbs can be connected without *and* or any other conjunction (serial verbs).					●	
LINKING VERBS The verb *be* is not required in all sentences. In some primary languages, it is implied in the adjective form. In others the concept is expressed as a verb.		●	●		●	●
PASSIVE VOICE Passive voice in the primary language does not require a helping verb.		●	●			●
TRANSITIVE VERBS VERSUS INTRANSITIVE VERBS Verbs that do and do not take a direct object differ between English and the primary language.	●		●	●		
PHRASAL VERBS Phrasal verbs do not exist in the primary language. There is often confusion over their meaning in English.	●					
HAVE **VERSUS** *BE* Some Spanish constructions use *have* where English uses *be*.	●					

Grammatical Features

GRAMMAR POINT	SPANISH	VIETNAMESE	CANTONESE OR MANDARIN	PILIPINO OR TAGALOG	HMONG	KOREAN
Adjectives						
WORD ORDER Adjectives commonly come after nouns in the primary language.	●	●			●	
Adjectives always come before words they modify in the primary language.			●			
COMPARISON Comparative and superlative are usually formed with separate words in the primary language, the equivalent of *more* and *most* in English.	●				●	●
CONFUSION OF *-ING* AND *-ED* FORMS The speakers of the primary language sometimes confuse these adjective forms, not distinguishing between *an interesting movie* and *an interested viewer*, for example.	●	●	●	●	●	●
Adverbs						
Adverbs usually come before verbs in the primary language, and this tendency is carried over into English.			●			
Prepositions						
English prepositions do not match the prepositions of the primary language precisely.	●	●	●	●	●	●
Complex Sentences						
The primary language lacks tense markers so that matching the tenses of two verbs in one sentence correctly can be difficult. Learners may also try to analyze the tense needed in English according to meaning, which in some cases can result in the use of an incorrect tense.		●	●	●	●	
IF* VERSUS *WHEN The primary language has one expression that covers the use of English *if* and *when* for the future.				●		

Grammatical Features

GRAMMAR POINT	SPANISH	VIETNAMESE	CANTONESE OR MANDARIN	PILIPINO OR TAGALOG	HMONG	KOREAN
Sentence Structure						
The pattern in the primary language is to describe what happens first while later occurrences follow. This is not an error in English, but it leads to a lack of sentence variety.			●			
The phrase with the indirect object can come before the direct object in Spanish.	●					
Spanish requires double negatives in many sentence structures.	●					
Questions						
The primary language doesn't use subject-verb inversion in questions.		●	●	●		●
In the primary language, word order is the same in some questions and statements, depending on the context.			●	●	●	●
In the primary language, there is no exact counterpart to the *do/did* verb in questions.	●			●	●	●
YES/NO QUESTIONS In the primary language, learners tend to answer yes by repeating the verb in the question. They tend to say no by using *not* and repeating the verb.			●		●	
TAG QUESTIONS The primary language has no exact counterpart to a tag question, forms them differently, or does not add *do/did* to questions.		●	●			●

Glossary

academic language The language of school and texts; words, sentence structures, and discourse structures that are not common in everyday speech.

accuracy A measure of a student's decoding skill, often expressed as the number of words read correctly per minute (WCPM).

affective filter In language-acquisition theory, negative feelings such as anxiety or disengagement that can obstruct a learner's efforts to acquire a new language.

anchor text A text that serves as a cornerstone of an instructional lesson or unit and a springboard for discussion and learning; a text that is worthy of close reading and rereading.

automaticity The ability to recognize words quickly and easily so that the reader's attention is focused on the meaning of the text.

benchmark assessment An assessment that is cumulative in nature and serves to measure students' progress against medium- or long-term goals.

blending The combining of individual speech-sounds into words. Blending may be practiced orally only, as a phonemic-awareness skill, or in conjunction with letter-sound knowledge, to decode written words.

choral reading A method of fluency practice in which groups of students, and often the teacher, read aloud simultaneously.

close reading Reading attentively and skillfully to examine key ideas and details, to analyze author's craft, and to integrate knowledge and ideas.

cognate A word that is similar in form and meaning to a word in another language; for example, the English *gratitude* and the Spanish *gratitud* are cognates.

collaborative writing Writing instruction in which students build on each other's ideas and efforts to develop joint compositions.

comprehensible input In language-acquisition theory, language that a student can understand even without understanding each individual word or language structure; common techniques for ensuring comprehensible input include using objects, gestures, or visuals to support the language of instruction.

comprehension The construction of meaning through interaction with a text.

content knowledge Knowledge about topics studied in content areas such as science, mathematics, reading and language arts, and social studies; knowledge of concepts, ideas, and facts, as opposed to command of words and language structures.

culturally responsive teaching Instruction in which the teacher respects and leverages students' cultural knowledge, frames of reference, and experiences to make learning more appropriate, engaging, and relevant.

decodable text Text used for decoding practice, in which the majority of words contain only previously taught letter-sound relationships; in a decodable text, any words that students cannot be expected to decode have been pretaught as high-frequency words or as "story words" (words that are needed for a particular story or text).

decoding Using knowledge of letter-sound correspondences to convert written words into spoken words.

domain-specific vocabulary Specialized vocabulary that usually relates to a content area, or domain, such as biology or mathematics.

echo reading A method of fluency practice in which the teacher reads aloud manageable chunks of text, modeling proper phrasing and expression, and has students repeat.

explicit instruction Teaching that is clear, straightforward, and directly stated. Steps of explicit instruction include direct explanation, modeling, guided practice, independent practice, formative assessment, and corrective feedback.

fix-up strategies Steps a reader takes to correct comprehension problems, such as restating the text in his or her own words, rereading, or reading ahead.

fluency The ability to read orally with speed, accuracy, and expression; silent reading that is fast and accurate and yields good comprehension.

formative assessment Assessment that is designed to inform adjustments in instruction by providing information about what students know and can do and what they still need to learn.

foundational skills The skills that form the foundation, or first support, for reading achievement: print concepts, phonological awareness (including phonemic awareness), phonics and word recognition, and fluency.

grapheme The letter or combination of letters that stand for a single sound. A grapheme can be a single letter, such as *n* or *e*, or more than one letter, such as *ck*.

guided practice Guidance, assistance, and feedback provided to students as they learn and practice using a strategy or skill.

guiding question A question that inspires inquiry and helps students focus their efforts as they analyze, synthesize, and discuss what they are reading.

high-frequency words The most common words in written English. Many high-frequency words, such as *come*, *does*, *give*, and *the*, have uncommon letter-sound correspondences but must be instantly recognized by beginning readers if they are to read connected text; these words are taught, practiced, and reviewed systematically.

idiomatic expression A combination of words that is understood by native speakers to have a special, nonliteral meaning; examples: *stepping up to the plate*; *feeling blue*; *on top of the world*.

informal assessment Using ongoing observations of students to monitor their progress and evaluate the need for additional instruction and practice.

language proficiency level The stage of English language development; in this program, English language students are identified as Emerging, Expanding, or Bridging.

language domains In language-acquisition theory, the four domains of language are often identified as speaking, listening, reading, and writing.

language function The main job of a particular language form or pattern; example: the function of the pattern "these things are alike because . . . " is to compare.

linguistic transfer The generalization of knowledge from one language to another. Positive transfer occurs when a student can apply what he or she knows in the first, or native, language to the second, or target, language; using cognates to relate words in the second language to words in the first language is an example of positive transfer.

mentor text A text that serves as a model or inspiration for student writing.

metacognition Awareness of one's thinking process; awareness of what one understands and does not understand; "thinking about thinking."

modeling Demonstrating the reasoning and mental processes involved in applying a strategy; "thinking aloud."

morphology The study of the meaningful parts of words and how they are put together.

multiple-meaning word Words that have more than one distinct meaning and more than one entry in a dictionary.

Glossary

multi-tiered system of supports (MTSS) A systematic, data-driven, coordinated approach to meeting students' individual needs with high-quality first instruction, appropriate supports, and intervention at various intensity levels. A strong MTSS is based on high-quality professional development for teachers and a culture that integrates strong leadership with teacher empowerment.

oral vocabulary Words understood and used in listening and speaking; a student's oral vocabulary consists of the words he or she can understand when listening and can use when speaking.

partner reading Reading aloud with a partner who gives feedback and assistance with word identification.

performance task Generally, a learning and assessment activity that exercises higher-level thinking and real-world problem solving and that involves multiple steps, domains, or standards; specific assessments may have specific requirements for performance tasks.

phoneme The smallest sound in spoken language. The word *neck* has three phonemes: /n/, /e/, and /k/.

phonics The system of instruction that focuses on letter-sound correspondences to enable beginning readers to "sound out" and spell words.

productive language Words and language structures that students can produce, or use, in speaking and writing.

progress monitoring The practice of assessing students' academic performance periodically in order to 1) evaluate the effectiveness of instruction; 2) create more effective programs to meet the needs of individual students; and 3) estimate rates of student improvement.

prosody The qualities of speech that make it expressive, including changes in tone and rhythm.

rate The speed at which a student reads, often expressed as words per minute (WPM).

read aloud A selection that is read out loud to students, often accompanied by teacher modeling.

receptive language Words and language structures that students can understand in listening and reading.

register The variety of a language used in a particular setting or for a particular purpose.

repeated reading A method of fluency practice in which students read and reread a text until they can read it with speed, accuracy, and expression.

scaffolding Temporary guidance or support provided by the teacher to a student who needs additional assistance to complete a task or master an objective; the goal is to build student's capacity for mastering the skill on his or her own in the future.

sentence frame A scaffolding tool to help students, often English learners, produce complete and expanded sentences; in a sentence frame, key parts of the sentence are omitted for the student to fill in.

sentence unpacking Analyzing a complex or interesting sentence by breaking it into parts and identifying the meaningful elements of each part.

summative assessment An assessment that provides information for evaluating the success of an instructional program by measuring students' achievement and growth at the end of a relatively long-term instructional period.

synthesis Combining knowledge and ideas from two or more sources or experiences to arrive at a higher level of understanding.

text complexity A measure of the overall level of challenge that a given text presents; text complexity can be measured quantitatively (as with readability programs); qualitatively (by analyzing the text for unfamiliar content and language); and in relation to the reader and the task (by considering how engaging, relevant, and accessible the text would be for a specific audience and purpose).

text-dependent question A question that can be answered by referring to information and ideas that are present in the text being discussed.

text evidence Support lifted directly from text to support inferences, claims, and assertions. Examples of text evidence include direct quotations from a text as well as summaries, paraphrases, and images that accompany a text.

text structure How the information within a written text is organized. Examples include cause-effect, problem-solution, and comparison-contrast.

think aloud A teaching technique in which the teacher uses a monologue to demonstrate thinking and reasoning processes; a method for modeling the use of a strategy or strategies.

think-pair-share A learning strategy in which students collaborate to solve a problem or answer a question about an assignment. Students think about a topic or answer to a question, and then share ideas with classmates. Partner discussions encourage all students' participation, focus attention, and enhance student comprehension.

total physical response (TPR) A language instruction strategy that involves giving commands in the target language and having students respond through physical action.

traits of writing Characteristics of good writing, organized in categories useful for assessment and instruction: ideas, organization, voice, word choice, sentence structure, and conventions.

twenty-first century skills The cognitive as well as social skills and dispositions that will enable students to succeed in the dynamic, fast-paced, and complex world of the 21st century. While several frameworks exist, most include skills related to global or cultural awareness, appreciation of diversity, and collaboration with others.

universal access A concept or schema utilizing strategies for planning for the widest variety of learners.

Universal Design for Learning (UDL) A set of principles guiding curriculum development that gives all students equal opportunity to learn. Teachers base their plans on students' needs as they consider different ways to present information; different ways students can express what they know; and different ways of nurturing student motivation.

Houghton Mifflin Harcourt

JOURNEYS

Every Student

Empowered. Inspired. Confident.

In every unit, students learn a variety of writing skills and forms that develop proficiency with the writing mode.

Students write to sources every week!

Performance Task

WRITE ABOUT READING

Response By the time he was in the eighth grade, Cesar Chavez had worked on his family's own ranch as well as on land owned by others. Write a paragraph explaining how these experiences prepared him to fight for farmworkers' rights. Include text evidence from the selection that helps to explain the effect his childhood experiences had on him.

Writing Tip

As you write your response, stay focused on the topic. Prepare to write by identifying relevant experiences from Cesar's childhood. Use prepositional phrases to add interesting information to your response.

Lesson 19

ANCHOR TEXT

Harvesting Hope

☑ **GENRE**

A **biography** tells about a person's life and is written by another person. As you read, look for:

► information about why the person is important
► opinions and personal judgments based on facts
► events in time order

MEET THE AUTHOR

Kathleen Krull

As a teenager, Kathleen Krull was fired from her part-time job at the library for reading too much! When she went on to become an author, she found a job that would allow her to read as much as she wanted. Known for her history books and biographies, she has written about presidents, scientists, writers, musicians, and athletes.

MEET THE ILLUSTRATOR

Yuyi Morales

Yuyi Morales was born in Xalapa, Mexico. As a child she wanted to be an acrobat. Today she is a writer and an illustrator, and her books have been published in English and Spanish. Not all of her artwork is done on paper. She also makes puppets.

GUIDE TO
JOURNEYS WRITING
FOCUS ON GENRE INSTRUCTION

UNIT 1: NARRATIVE WRITING

	Day 1	Day 2	Day 3	Day 4	Day 5
Lesson 1 *Descriptive Writing*	**Introduce the Model** (T52) Projectable	**Focus Trait: Elaboration** Connect to Literature, Reader's Notebook	**Prewrite** *Planning a Descriptive Paragraph, Projectable*	**Draft** *Using Web (Day 3)*	**Revise and Edit** *Analyze the Model* **Interactive Lessons,** Projectable, Student Book, Writing Checklist/Rubric
Lesson 2 *Story*	**Introduce the Model** (T128) Projectable	**Focus Trait: Purpose** Connect to Literature, Reader's Notebook	**Prewrite** *Planning a Story, Projectable*	**Draft** *Using Flow Chart (Day 3)*	**Revise and Edit** *Analyze the Model* **Interactive Lessons,** Projectable, Student Book, Writing Checklist/Rubric
Lesson 3 *Dialogue*	**Introduce the Model** (T206) Projectable	**Focus Trait: Conventions** Connect to Literature, Reader's Notebook	**Prewrite** *Planning a Dialogue, Projectable/GO*	**Draft** *Using Column Map (Day 3)*	**Revise and Edit** *Analyze the Model* **Interactive Lessons,** Projectable, Student Book, Writing Checklist/Rubric
Lesson 4 *Reading/Writing Workshop, Fictional Narrative*	**Analyze the Model** (T280) Projectable	**Focus Trait: Organization** Connect to Literature, Reader's Notebook	**Prewrite** *Exploring a Topic*	**Prewrite** *Planning a Fictional Narrative, Connect to Literature, Projectable*	**Prewrite** *Analyze the Model* **Interactive Lessons,** Planning a Fictional Narrative, Student Book
Lesson 5 *Reading/Writing Workshop, Fictional Narrative*	**Draft** (T358) *Using Story Map (Lesson 4), Connect to Literature*	**Draft Focus Trait: Conventions** Connect to Literature, Reader's Notebook	**Draft** *Transitions, Connect to Literature*	**Revise** Connect to Literature, Writing Conference Form	**Revise, Edit, and Publish** Student Book, Writing Checklist/Rubric

PERFORMANCE ASSESSMENT   Unit 4: Narrative Essay

UNIT 2: INFORMATIVE WRITING

	Day 1	Day 2	Day 3	Day 4	Day 5
Lesson 6 *News Report*	**Introduce the Model** (T52) Projectable	**Focus Trait: Organization** Connect to Literature, Reader's Notebook	**Prewrite** *Planning a News Report, Projectable*	**Draft** *Using a T Map (Day 3)*	**Revise and Edit** *Analyze the Model* **Interactive Lessons,** Projectable, Student Book, Writing Checklist/Rubric
Lesson 7 *Information Paragraph*	**Introduce the Model** (T126) Projectable	**Focus Trait: Evidence** Connect to Literature, Reader's Notebook	**Prewrite** *Planning a Paragraph, Projectable*	**Draft** *Using Web (Day 3)*	**Revise and Edit** *Analyze the Model* **Interactive Lessons,** Projectable, Student Book, Writing Checklist/Rubric
Lesson 8 *Book Report*	**Introduce the Model** (T202) Projectable	**Focus Trait: Purpose** Connect to Literature, Reader's Notebook	**Prewrite** *Planning a Book Report, Projectable*	**Draft** *Using Chart (Day 3)*	**Revise and Edit** *Analyze the Model* **Interactive Lessons,** Projectable, Student Book, Writing Checklist/Rubric
Lesson 9 *Reading/Writing Workshop, Explanatory Essay*	**Analyze the Model** (T276) Projectable	**Focus Trait: Evidence** Connect to Literature, Reader's Notebook	**Prewrite** *Exploring a Topic, Connect to Literature, Create Chart*	**Prewrite** *Planning an Explanatory Essay, Projectable*	**Prewrite** *Analyze the Model* **Interactive Lessons,** Planning an Exploratory Essay, Student Book
Lesson 10 *Reading/Writing Workshop, Explanatory Essay*	**Draft** (T350) *Using Graphic Organizer (Lesson 9)*	**Draft Focus Trait: Elaboration** Connect to Literature, Reader's Notebook,	**Draft** *Domain Specific Vocabulary, Connect to Literature*	**Revise** Connect to Literature, Writing Conference Form	**Revise, Edit, and Publish** Student Book, Writing Checklist/Rubric

PERFORMANCE ASSESSMENT   Unit 2: Informative Essay

*Additional writing support provided daily in the Common Core Writing Handbook (CCWH).

UNIT 3: OPINION (ARGUMENTATIVE) WRITING

	Day 1	Day 2	Day 3	Day 4	Day 5
Lesson 11 *Persuasive Paragraph*	**Introduce the Model** (T52) *Projectable*	**Focus Trait: Purpose** *Connect to Literature, Reader's Notebook*	**Prewrite** *Planning a Persuasive Paragraph, Projectable*	**Draft** *Using Web* (Day 3)	**Revise and Edit** *Analyze the Model* **Interactive Lessons,** *Projectable, Student Book, Writing Checklist/Rubric*
Lesson 12 *Problem/Solution Composition*	**Introduce the Model** (T126) *Projectable*	**Focus Trait: Organization** *Connect to Literature, Reader's Notebook*	**Prewrite** *Planning a Problem/ Solution Composition, Projectable*	**Draft** *Using Problem/ Solution Chart* (Day 3)	**Revise and Edit** *Analyze the Model* **Interactive Lessons,** *Projectable, Student Book, Writing Checklist/Rubric*
Lesson 13 *Persuasive Letter*	**Introduce the Model** (T206) *Projectable*	**Focus Trait: Evidence** *Connect to Literature, Reader's Notebook*	**Prewrite** *Planning a Persuasive Letter, Projectable*	**Draft** *Using Web* (Day 3)	**Revise and Edit** *Analyze the Model* **Interactive Lessons,** *Projectable, Student Book, Writing Checklist/Rubric*
Lesson 14 *Reading/Writing Workshop, Persuasive Essay*	**Analyze the Model** (T282) *Projectable*	*Focus Trait: Purpose Connect to Literature, Reader's Notebook*	**Prewrite** *Exploring a Topic, 5 W's Chart*	**Prewrite** *Planning a Persuasive Essay, Projectable, Idea-Support Map*	**Prewrite** **Interactive Lessons,** *Planning a Persuasive Essay, Student Book, Idea-Support Map*
Lesson 15 *Reading/Writing Workshop, Persuasive Essay*	**Draft** (T356) *Use Graphic Organizers from Lesson 14*	**Draft Focus Trait: Conventions** *Connect to Literature, Reader's Notebook*	**Draft** *Connotation*	**Revise** *Connect to Literature, Writing Conference Form*	**Revise, Edit, and Publish** *Student Book, Writing Checklist/Rubric*

PERFORMANCE ASSESSMENT   **Unit 1: Opinion Essay**

UNIT 4: NARRATIVE WRITING

	Day 1	Day 2	Day 3	Day 4	Day 5
Lesson 16 *Descriptive Paragraph*	**Introduce the Model** (T52) *Projectable*	**Focus Trait: Development** *Connect to Literature, Reader's Notebook*	**Prewrite** *Planning a Descriptive Paragraph, Projectable*	**Draft** *Using Web* (Day 3)	**Revise and Edit** *Analyze the Model* **Interactive Lessons,** *Projectable, Student Book, Writing Checklist/Rubric*
Lesson 17 *Friendly Letter*	**Introduce the Model** (T126) *Projectable*	**Focus Trait: Purpose** *Connect to Literature, Reader's Notebook*	**Prewrite** *Planning a Friendly Letter, Projectable*	**Draft** *Using Flow Chart* (Day 3)	**Revise and Edit** *Analyze the Model* **Interactive Lessons,** *Projectable, Student Book, Writing Checklist/Rubric*
Lesson 18 *Story*	**Introduce the Model** (T204) *Projectable*	**Focus Trait: Elaboration** *Connect to Literature, Reader's Notebook*	**Prewrite** *Planning a Story, Projectable*	**Draft** *Using Flow Chart* (Day 3)	**Revise and Edit** *Analyze the Model* **Interactive Lessons,** *Projectable, Student Book, Writing Checklist/Rubric*
Lesson 19 *Reading/Writing Workshop, Personal Narrative*	**Analyze the Model** (T278) *Projectable*	**Focus Trait: Organization** *Connect to Literature, Reader's Notebook*	**Prewrite** *Exploring a Topic*	**Prewrite** *Planning a Personal Narrative, Projectable*	**Prewrite** **Interactive Lessons,** *Planning a Personal Narrative, Student Book, Event Chart*
Lesson 20 *Reading/Writing Workshop, Personal Narrative*	**Draft** (T356) *Connect to Literature, Use Completed Charts from Lesson 4*	**Draft Focus Trait: Conventions** *Reader's Notebook*	**Draft** *Elaboration, Connect to Literature*	**Revise** *Connect to Literature*	**Revise, Edit, and Publish** *Student Book, Writing Checklist/Rubric*

PERFORMANCE ASSESSMENT   **Unit 5: Mixed Practice • Task 4: Narrative**

Writing to Sources can be found with every Performance Task in myWriteSmart.

UNIT 5: INFORMATIVE WRITING

	Day 1	Day 2	Day 3	Day 4	Day 5
Lesson 21 *Summary*	**Introduce the Model** (T54) Projectable	**Focus Trait:** Evidence *Connect to Literature, Reader's Notebook*	**Prewrite** *Planning a Summary, Projectable*	**Draft** *Using Story Map* (Day 3)	**Revise and Edit** *Analyze the Model* **Interactive Lessons,** Projectable, Student Book, Writing Checklist/ Rubric
Lesson 22 *Explanation*	**Introduce the Model** (T130) Projectable	**Focus Trait:** Elaboration *Connect to Literature, Reader's Notebook*	**Prewrite** *Planning an Explanation, Projectable*	**Draft** *Using T Map* (Day 3)	**Revise and Edit** *Analyze the Model* **Interactive Lessons,** Projectable, Student Book, Writing Checklist/Rubric
Lesson 23 *Procedural Composition*	**Introduce the Model** (T208) Projectable	**Focus Trait:** Organization *Connect to Literature, Reader's Notebook*	**Prewrite** *Planning a Procedural Composition, Projectable*	**Draft** *Using Flow Chart* (Day 3)	**Revise and Edit** *Analyze the Model* **Interactive Lessons,** Projectable, Student Book, Writing Checklist/Rubric
Lesson 24 *Reading/Writing Workshop, Research Report*	**Analyze the Model** (T282) Projectable	**Focus Trait:** Purpose *Connect to Literature, Reader's Notebook*	**Prewrite** *Exploring a Topic*	**Prewrite** *Planning a Research Report, Connect to Literature, Projectable*	**Prewrite** **Interactive Lessons,** Planning a Research Report, Student Book
Lesson 25 *Reading/Writing Workshop, Research Report*	**Draft** (T356) *Student Writing Model*	**Draft** **Focus Trait: Elaboration** *Connect to Literature, Reader's Notebook*	**Draft** *Using Sources, Student Writing Model*	**Revise** *Word Choice, Connect to Literature, Student Model*	**Revise, Edit, and Publish** *Student Book, Writing Checklist/ Rubric*

PERFORMANCE ASSESSMENT　　**Unit 5: Mixed Practice • Task 2: Informative Essay**

UNIT 6: OPINION (ARGUMENTATIVE) WRITING

	Day 1	Day 2	Day 3	Day 4	Day 5
Lesson 26 *Response to Fiction*	**Introduce the Model** (T42) Projectable	**Focus Trait:** Evidence *Connect to Literature, Reader's Notebook*	**Prewrite** *Planning a Summary, Projectable*	**Draft** *Using Story Map* (Day 3)	**Revise and Edit** *Analyze the Model* **Interactive Lessons,** Projectable, Student Book, Writing Checklist/Rubric
Lesson 27 *Journal Entry*	**Introduce the Model** (T130) Projectable	**Focus Trait:** Elaboration *Connect to Literature, Reader's Notebook*	**Prewrite** *Planning an Explanation, Projectable*	**Draft** *Using T Map* (Day 3)	**Revise and Edit** *Analyze the Model* **Interactive Lessons,** Projectable, Student Book, Writing Checklist/ Rubric
Lesson 28 *Public Service Announcement*	**Introduce the Model** (T208) Projectable	**Focus Trait:** Organization *Connect to Literature, Reader's Notebook*	**Prewrite** *Planning a Procedural Composition, Projectable*	**Draft** *Using Flow Chart* (Day 3)	**Revise and Edit** *Analyze the Model* **Interactive Lessons,** Projectable, Student Book, Writing Checklist/ Rubric
Lesson 29 *Opinion Essay*	**Analyze the Model** (T282) Projectable	**Focus Trait:** Organization *Connect to Literature, Reader's Notebook*	**Prewrite** *Exploring a Topic*	**Prewrite** *Planning a Research Report, Connect to Literature, Projectable*	**Prewrite** *Interactive Lessons, Planning a Research Report, Student Book*
Lesson 30 *Opinion Essay*	**Draft** (T356) *Student Writing Model*	**Draft** **Focus Trait:** Conventions *Connect to Literature, Reader's Notebook*	**Draft** *Using Sources, Student Writing Model*	**Revise** *Word Choice, Connect to Literature, Student Model*	**Revise, Edit, and Publish** *Student Book, Writing Checklist/Rubric*

PERFORMANCE ASSESSMENT　　**Unit 5: Mixed Practice • Task 1: Opinion Essay**

Connect with us:
 🐦 📘 in 📌 YouTube

Writing to Sources can be found with every Performance Task in myWriteSmart.
*Additional writing support provided daily in the Common Core Writing Handbook (CCWH).

hmhco.com • 800.225.54

Houghton
Mifflin
Harcourt.